MADISON COUNTY TENNESSEE

HISTORY
AND
BIOGRAPHIES

Goodspeed

Heritage Books
2024

HERITAGE BOOKS

AN IMPRINT OF HERITAGE BOOKS, INC.

Books, CDs, and more—Worldwide

For our listing of thousands of titles see our website
at
www.HeritageBooks.com

A Facsimile Reprint
Published 2024 by
HERITAGE BOOKS, INC.
Publishing Division
5810 Ruatan Street
Berwyn Heights, MD 20740

Originally published:
Chicago and Nashville
The Goodspeed Publishing Co.,
1887

— Publisher's Notice —
In reprints such as this, it is often not possible to remove
blemishes from the original. We feel the contents of this
book warrant its reissue despite these blemishes and
hope you will agree and read it with pleasure.

International Standard Book Number
Paperbound: 978-0-7884-9197-9

MADISON COUNTY.

MADISON COUNTY lies on the plateau or slope between the basin of the Tennessee and the Mississippi. It is at the headwaters of the Forked Deer, and lies near the water-shed between the two large rivers above named. The surface of the county in general is level or undulating. This is particularly the case in the center and toward the north and the west. To find rolling or broken lands, the east and south, where the surface is quite broken, must be looked to.

The streams of the county are all comparatively small, shallow and sluggish. With the exception of Big Black and Clover Creeks, which are tributaries of the Hatchie, the streams all belong to the Forked Deer system. Middle Fork, of Forked Deer, enters the county from Carroll near the northeast corner of the county, and passes southwesterly through the county and enters Gibson County about sixteen miles northwest from Jackson. South Fork, of Forked Deer, enters what was the southeast corner of the county, and passes in a western direction out of the county. Little Middle Fork enters Madison at a little south of the center on the eastern line of the county, and unites with South Fork about four miles east of Jackson. Greer Creek is a small tributary of Little Middle Fork. Turkey, Jones, Johnson and Cub Creeks are tributaries of South Fork. Dyer Creek, which rises about two miles north of Jackson, empties into Middle Fork of Forked Deer River. From their shallow beds these streams are subject to frequent overflows. Mill sites have been established on the more favorable of these streams since the organization of the county.

The soil of the county is generally of a dark color, having a mixture of clay and sand. In the northern and western sections it is more of a yellowish tinge, while in the southern and eastern sections it has a reddish tinge, owing to the admixture of iron oxides. The main body of the county rests on beds of orange sand. The formations are all comparatively recent, no portion reaching as far back as the silurian, and is largely of alluvial formation. As would be expected the soil is generally very productive, and stands drought and other extremes remarkably well. In consequence of sluggish streams, alluvial beds and vegetable sediment, there are considerable malarial troubles in the summer and fall, but these are not generally of a serious character. The character of the soil does not indicate any great deal of mineral wealth, as almost the entire formation is of the quaternary period, and consequently too modern for the carbonaceous, argillaceous or auriferous deposits, although ferruginous sandstones are found in some parts of the county, near which are some chalybeate springs.

Although formerly well supplied with timber there is now no great abundance for export. Formerly there were large quantities of poplar (*Lyriodendron tulipifera*), but its great value led to its destruction in a great measure. Perhaps the most valuable timber now left is the oak (*Quercus*). There are several varieties of the oak, which need no description, such as the white oak (*Quercus alba*), black oak (*Quercus tinctoria*), post oak (*Quercus obtusiloba*) and the black (Jack) oak (*Quercus nigra*). There are also large quantities of hickory (*Carya*) of several varieties, consisting of the common hickory (*Carya tormentosa*), the scaly bark hickory (*Carya alba*) and other varieties. There are the elm (*Ulmus*), the gum (*Nyssa*), both the sweet (*Liquidamber styraciflua*) and the black (*Nyssa aquatica*) or tupello, the beech (*Fagus ferruginea*), the ash (*Fraxinus*), maple (*Acer*), mulberry (*Morus*), black walnut (*Juglans nigra*), and many other of the less valuable timbers.

Though well suited for a wide variety of products the lower portions of the lands are devoted to the growth of cotton. A very heavy yield of this staple is obtained. The cereals are grown only to a limited extent. Vegetables grow well; the sandy character of the soil renders it well suited for the growth of all of the tuberous character. Timothy and clover do well, and thus render stock raising profitable. More of a mixed farming would doubtless yield a more certain and better income to husbandmen. The excellent facilities for transportation to the best markets are rapidly developing the industries of the county.

Madison County has an area of about 531 square miles, and an elevation of 400 feet above the sea. The first settlers of the County were mainly from Middle Tennessee; these, however, had come originally from Virginia and North Carolina, some from South Carolina. On the extinguishment of the titles of the Chickasaw Indians, in 1818–21, these pioneers, moved by the feelings that "westward the course of empire takes its way," soon again started to find new homes. The constant streams from the older States, pouring into and through Middle Tennessee, carried with them many who had found homes in the rich lands of Middle Tennessee. Moved by the restless tide of emigration, and incited by the rich fields in West Tennessee now unoccupied, many fell in with the current and were carried westward. In a few years after the opening of the country for settlement almost the entire portion of West Tennessee was covered with toiling thousands of a busy throng. Since the tide all originated from the same place the character of the people was very much alike. The intelligence, refinement, courteous bearing, high moral integrity, found in the Carolinas and Virginia, had their counterpart here. Closely related by marriage, social and business relations, the people of Tennessee have maintained their individual characteristics larger and more distinct than most any other people. There is here a homogeneity that is quite foreign to the Northern and Western States.

The first settlers came to Madison County in 1819–20. Adam R. Alexander, who had charge of the land office for the Tenth District, settled about two miles northwest of Jackson. His place was formerly called Alexandria. He not only held the land office, but was also a justice of the peace. Robert H. Dyer, who was one of the first justices, also settled not far from Alexander's place. Joseph Lynn, one of the commissioners for the organization of the county opened a farm about three miles west of Jackson. John T. Porter, one of the first commissioners, after the organization became the first register of the county. He lived near South Fork about three miles west of Jackson. Near Porter lived James Brown. Near Alexandria lived J. H. Raygin, a brother-in-law of Alexander. About five miles west of Jackson, beyond South Fork, James Cockrell settled with his family in September, 1821. W. G. Cockrell, his son, is now the efficient county superintendent. On the south side of Forked Deer were Frank Herron, Henning Pace and Benjamin Blythe; also Foster and Richard Golden, whose place was put in nomination for the county seat. On Johnson Creek were Benjamin Blythe, before mentioned, John and James McClish, Wm. Cooper, Nathaniel Robinson and Thomas Lacey. In the vicinity of Denmark, Thomas and Richard Sanders settled in 1822. Col. Williamson settled on Big Black some time during the same year. James M. Jelks settled northwest of Jackson in 1821. In the same neighborhood were the Mitchells and others. In a short time there was a settlement sufficient for a school. A log school-house was built in that neighborhood in 1822, which was standing a few years ago. A man named Tyner was the pioneer teacher.

Some time in 1820 Mr. Wear settled in the northeast part of the county, where he planted his first crop. In the vicinity of Cotton Grove were John Hardgrove, who was one of the commissioners of Jackson, the two McIvers, Duncan and Roderick, Elijah Jones, John and Thomas Brown, William Woodfork, an early magistrate, Stephen Cypert, George Todd and —— Vaulx. Adam Huntsman, the well known one-legged lawyer, lived about four miles east of Jackson; Nathan Deberry about the same distance. Wm. E. Butler, the well known trader and influential citizen, settled near the spring, where the water-works now stand, in 1819 or 1820. John McNairy, Joseph Phillips and Wm. E. Butler owned the lands east of Market Street, on which the city of Jackson now stands. The land lying immediately west of Market Street was owned by Thomas Shannon. James Trousdale settled between Jackson and Denmark in 1822. Charles Sevier, who was a hatter by trade, lived at first near Jackson, but afterward moved to the south side of the South Fork of Forked Deer River. Jacob Hill also settled south of the river. John Montgomery, Martin Lawrence, Lewis and Moses Needham, Francis Taylor, Jacob Thomas, Wm. Davis and John Tidwell all settled north of Jackson. In addition to these the following had settled in the county before 1824: Herndon and Vincent Haralson, Samuel Taylor, Wm. Atchison, George White, John Fare, or Farr, Elijah Jones, Wm. H. Doak, Henry L. Coulter, Smith Sullivan, Guy Smith, James Dollard, Zachariah Thomas, Wm. Davis, David Jernigen, James Caldwell, Nathan Simpson, C. C. Collier, Z. B. McCoy, Gabriel Chandler, S. D. Waddel, George Gentry, Wm. Harrison, Wm. Harris, Jacob Bradberry, David Jarrett, Rufus F. King, Wm. C. Love, Martin Cartmell, J. B. Hogg, Hazael Hewett, Michael Murchison, James Greer, David Ferguson, Bartholomew G. Stewart, J. S. Caruthers, Wm. Wilborn, H. L. Gray, Thomas Boling, James McDaniel, James Epps, William Witherspoon, William Harper, Cullen Lane, —— Exum, William Stephens and Phillip Alson.

Capt. Bates, now of the Sixteenth District, is said to have assisted in building the first court house in 1822. The first marriage in the county was between R. S. Jones and Canada H. Curtis. The ceremony was performed by A. R. Alexander, January 1, 1822. Samuel Jones, son of Elijah Jones, is said to have been the first child born in the county. —— Robertson, born at the house of Charles Sevier during a temporary sojourn of the parents, was the first child born in Jackson. A daughter of Samuel Swan, a small grocer, was the first female child. Jesse Russel came to the county in January, 1823, and his marriage, which occurred a few months afterward, was the first marriage in Jackson. Robert Russell, son of Jesse, was the first male child of a permanent resident. John Brown, a prominent lawyer of Jackson, son of Dr. John F. Brown, is but a few months younger than Rob. Russell. Col. Robt. I. Chester, born in North Carolina in 1793, came to Washington County in 1796, and to Madison County in 1823. He is still vigorous at ninety-four.

The early settlers had few of the luxuries of life, but plenty of the substantial things. Corn furnished most of the "staff of life." This was eaten as hominy, or made into meal, by beating in a mortar, grinding in a hand-mill, or a small water-mill. James Cockrell brought the first hand-mill to the county in September, 1821 This served not only for his own family, but also for his neighbors. One of the Jameses built the first mill on Wallick Creek, near Cotton Grove, in 1821. This mill had a capacity of five bushels per day, or ten bushels in twenty-four hours. A. R. Alexander built a mill on his land in 1822; Duncan McIver one on his land on Jones Creek, and Ezekiel McCoy one on Trace Creek, also in 1822. In 1823 George W. Still built a mill on his forty acre tract, on Trace Creek, Clark Spencer one on Cane Creek, T. J. Hardeman one on Pleasant Run, Obediah Mix one on Jones Creek, and Gabriel Chandler one on Young Creek; Col. Williamson built his mill on Big Black in February, 1823, and Newsom's mill, on Meredith Creek, was built in 1824. The rapid increase of population at this time brought about a rapid increase in the number of mills.

One of the Joneses built the first ferry, called Jones' Ferry, on South Fork, within the limits of the county, in 1820–21. This was west of Jackson. A ferry was established on South Fork, at Shannon's Landing, by Thomas Shannon, in 1822, also one on South Fork, by J. G. Caruthers, in the same year. A ferry was established by John Murray, on Hatchie, on his lands, in 1822, and one at Hatchie Bluff, by Wilson Jones. Ordinaries were opened by John Reding and Robert H. Dyer at their respective houses in 1822. The privilege of keeping an ordinary implied the privilege of selling liquors. Trade was carried on by wagon from Nashville. or by keel-boats, by way of the Forked Deer River. These boats brought flour, meat, coffee, sugar, domestics, etc., and carried away produce of various kinds. Barney Mitchell was for a long time owner of the principal line of boats. Newson perhaps brought the first boat, as he is known to have navigated South Fork in the spring of 1822. The corn crop of 1821 did not mature well, in consequence of which most of the bread stuff of that year had to be imported. It may be proper to remark here that little of Madison County's great staple cotton was raised during the first decade of its history, from the fact that it did not mature well. The virgin soil kept it growing too late without forcing it to maturity.

A short distance west of Jackson are several circular mounds of the usual form peculiar to Mound Builders. Near Pinson, in the southeast portion of the county on the Mobile & Ohio Railroad are several mounds of immense size. The highest of these is seventy-two feet in height and is of the usual conical shape. There are several others, fifty or more feet in height; some are almost perfect cones, others are frusta of cones, and one presents the frustum of a pentagonal pyramid, with sides seventy or more feet. In connection with these may be seen an old earthwork or earthworks. It consists of a ditch and an embankment, the embankment being from two to five feet in height. In some places two distinct embankments are to be seen extensively in parallel directions. The mounds consist of earthwork entirely and have been constructed of surface soil entirely. These mounds indicate that they have been built for defenses, for observatories or for sacred and sepulchral purposes. None but a few of the smaller ones have ever been examined with any care. Hon. J. G. Cisco, of the Forked Deer *Blade*, who is quite an antiquarian and who has an excellent collection of Indian relics, has made an examination of some of the smaller mounds and has been rewarded with a large number of arrow-heads, some excellent specimens of pottery and bones, skulls and other specimens of human remains. Charred remains, sticks, coals, bones are the usual relics of the sepulchral mounds. A scientific investigation, by some skillful antiquarian, of these mounds would doubtless reveal some rich pages of the history of a very peculiar people. A systematic boring and tunneling would amply repay the expenditure. A small appropriation each year expended under the direction of the State geologist, would add an immense treasure to Tennessee's archæological collection, which is being destroyed every year by the unlettered, or carried away by relic hunters from other States.

Madison County occupies almost the exact center of the western division of Tennessee. It is bounded on the north by Crockett, Gibson and Carroll Counties; on the east by Henderson and Chester; on the south by Chester and Hardeman; on the west by Haywood and Crockett Counties. It embraces an area of 340,000 acres.

The treaty of 1818 with the Chickasaw Indians allowed them the use of their lands as hunting grounds for two years, in consequence of which the settlements were not so rapid until after the limits of the treaty had expired. On November 9, 1821, the General Assembly at Murfreesboro passed an act providing for the organization of the western district into counties. It was under this act that Madison, Henry, Carroll and Henderson were created, but Madison was not finally organized till December 17, 1821. On Monday, December 17, 1821, the following commissioners met at the house of Adam R. Alexander, who lived about two miles west of Jackson, at what is now called the McClanahan farm, and who at the time was register of the land office for the tenth surveyor's district: B. tholomew G. Stewart, David Jarrett, William Atchison, Rob. H. D) John Thomas, Adam R. Alexander, Duncan McIver, Joseph Lynn, James Trousdale, Herndon Haralson, William Braden, Samuel Taylor and William Woodfork. The first step in the organization was the appointment of Robert Hughes, clerk, *pro tem.* The permanent officers then chosen were Roderick McIver, clerk; Thomas Shannon, sheriff; Herndon Haralson, chairman; John I. Porter, register; James Brown, ranger, and William Atchison, trustee. These men constituted the first county court. Joseph Lynn, Bartholomew Stewart and James Trousdale, with A. R. Alexander and John Hardgrove, in case of failure of the other parties, were selected by the General Assembly to determine the site for a seat of justice for the county, with power to erect public buildings. The places put in nomination were A. R. Alexander's place, Golden Station, three miles south of Jackson, and Jackson. The present site was agreed on May 19, 1822.

The court met at Alexander's residence until the September term 1822, when the first court house was ready for occupancy. This house was erected by John Houston for which he was allowed $135. This house stood on the square near the northeast corner and was a log building, one story high, covered with clapboards resting on ridge poles. This building was about 30x40 feet and stood till 1824–25, when the rapidly increasing population seemed to justify a new court house. The second house was a brick building two stories in height and about the same dimensions otherwise as the former house. This building was erected by Benjamin Gholson in the fall and winter of 1824–25. In addition to the court house, offices were erected on the square for the county officers. The county court clerk's office and registry office stood at the northeast corner of the square and the circuit clerk's office was at the southwest corner of the square. The court house was not a substantial building, and it became necessary to tear it down and erect a larger and more substantial building. Steps were taken as early as 1837 to erect the new building, but it was not till 1839 that the building was well under way. The committee consisted of J. W. Campbell, David Thompshire, Granberry Anderson, J. L. Talbot, Thomas Connally, Wm. Croan, R. W. May, I. W. Herron, James Caruthers, Wyatt Mooring and Samuel Lancaster. The contract was let to Thomas Brown, who was assisted by his brother, Robert Brown, who still resides in Jackson. The brick work was done by John and Thomas Norville, and the other work by the Browns. The dome and some of the painting were not completed till 1845. In 1839 the courts met at rooms at the Lafayette Inn, rents being charged for the same at $250 per year. The federal court met at the Presbyterian Church. The court house is a two-story building and is about 50x60 feet. It contains rooms for all the county offices, and a room for the various courts of the county, as well as a supreme court room. This building was erected at a total cost of about $25,000, and is in an excellent state of preservation.

On November 23, 1883, the United States Government purchased the block on the corner of Market and Baltimore Streets, for the purpose of erecting thereon a government building, to be used as a postoffice, federal court room, etc. The block was known as the "McCorry Block." Deeds were madeby H. W. and C. A. McCorry, Wm. A. Barnhill and wife, Caroline Barnhill, *et al.*, S. J. Caruthers and J. W. Gates, to the United States Government for the aggregate sum of $7,000. The building is about 50x60 feet. It is of the most approved architecture and finish. It is built of brick resting on a stone basement. The streets on its fronts are paved with fine curbing, and the lot enclosed by an iron fence. The entire cost of the building and fixtures amounts to about $100,000. It is by far the finest building in the city of Jackson.

The first public road ordered to be cut out in the county, was one to lead from the court house, to meet a contemplated road to be opened from the office (surveyor's), in the Ninth District, on the line of the county, near the northeast corner of Section 8, Range 2, by way of Duncan McIver's Mill on Jones Creek. The committee consisted of Duncan McIver, Herndon Haralson, George Todd, Ryland Chandler, Vincent Haralson and Roderick McIver. This order was passed December 19, 1819. On March 18, 1822, B. G. Stewart, Frances Taylor, Thomas Jones, Samuel Taylor and Jacob Bradberry, were ordered to open a road from the court house by way of the Forked Deer Postoffice and Francis Taylor's mill toward the center of Carroll County. At the same time Guy Smith, H. L. Gray, J. G. Caruthers, David Ferguson, J. B. Hogg, Moses Oldham and James Trousdale, were to open a road from where the above struck the Madison line along the ridge by way of Robert H. Dyer's and Caruthers' Ferry, the nearest route to McGuire's Ferry on Big Hatchie. Ezekiel A. McCoy, Duncan McIver, Wm. E. Butler, Vincent Haralson, Gabriel Chandler, Moses Wilson, Wm. Wilson, Martin Cartmell, John Jones, Hazael Hewett and Ryland Chandler were ordered at the same time to open the road from Jackson to the seat of Henderson County (Lexington). In September, 1822, the road leading from the "town of Alexandria" (*i. e.* Alexander's land office), was opened by D. Horton, Stokely D. Hays, Wm. H. Doak, Wm. E. Butler, John Harrison and Arthur F. Gray, to connect with the landing on the south fork of the Forked Deer River. Wm. Braden, Adam R. Alexander, J. G. Caruthers, Joel Dyer, J. T. Porter, David Jarrett, H. L. Gray, Thomas Boling and Guy Smith, were to open the road to Middle Fork. James Trousdale, N. J. Hay, Andrew Hay, Wm. Espy, James Tidwell, James Poor and George Meazler, were to open the road from Alexandria to Harrison's Bluff. The importance of having good communication between the different parts of the county was grasped at an early day, and the work accomplished without delay. The McClanahan Levee road, which leads from Jackson to Somerville, across the south fork of Forked Deer, was built by Dickens and Garrett in about 1835. This was a toll road, and for a time paid large dividends. The Chester Levee was named in honor of Col. R. I. Chester, who aided largely in its construction. Campbell's Levee was built at a later date, and leads from Jackson to Brownsville. All three of these roads are now under control of the county, by which they are kept in repair.

In 1852 aid from Madison County was asked for the construction of the Mobile & Ohio Railroad. In April of that year the county court, by a large majority, voted $100,000 stock to assist in the enterprise. Warrants to the amount of $50,000 were to be issued in 1856 and $50,000 in 1857. John C. M. Garland was made tax collector for the road. He was bound in the sum of $100,000 for the faithful performance of his duty, with Stephen Miller, A. S. Rogers, W. R. Collier, Hiram Johnson and George A. Connally as sureties. New tax collectors were appointed from year to year, as the bonds became due. The road was completed in due time after the issuance of the bonds. The Illinois Central was built a few years later than the Mobile & Ohio, and a few years ago was leased by the present company. It is a main thoroughfare from New Orleans to St. Louis and Chicago. The Brownsville & Jackson Railroad was chartered in September, 1882, by Napoleon Hill, W. H. Moore, Lois Hanamer, J. C. Neeley, J. R. Bond and W. P. Dunavant. It is intended to connect Brownsville, Haywood County, with Jackson, Madison County. The Ohio Valley Railroad was chartered in 1886, by J. W. Allison, J. L. Wisdom, W. P. Robertson, E. S. Mallory, of Madison, and J. J. Head, of Henry County. It is intended to connect some point on the northern line of the State with some point in Hardeman or McNairy, and to pass through the intermediate counties.

The first jail was ready for occupancy in December, 1822. This building stood south of the court house and was erected, at a cost of $95, by Samuel Shannon. In February, 1825, this old jail was offered for sale and a new one erected. The second one stood till about 1835, when a new brick jail was erected on the lot near where the present jail stands. In 1840 John Norville, Robert W. May and John Irvin were appointed a committee to improve and repair said jail. With the several improvements, this jail sufficed till the courts were closed by the war. This was then sold and became a private residence. In August, 1865, Greenberry, Anderson, Wm. Alexander, P. D. W. Conger, J. R. Chappell, J. M. C. Garland, Harvey Brown and J. S. Miller were appointed a committee to report on the propriety of building a new jail. The work was undertaken in 1866. Warrants on the county to the amount of $18,000 were issued for the purpose of building the same. The building stands on the old jail lot, and is a two-story structure, with cells on the second floor. It is a well built and creditable building. It is a brick structure, and contains not only the jail proper, with its prison cells, but the jailer's residence as well.

Previous to 1849, the poor of the county were farmed out to the lowest bidder, and were scattered over the county without system and with little regard to comfort and convenience. In the early part of the decade of 1840, a farm was purchased, with an eye to the erection of a poor-house thereon and collecting all paupers to the one place, but the one chosen did not prove a suitable location, and in 1841, Wyatt Mooring, John M. Barnett and John Irvin, were appointed by the county court to sell the same and to purchase a new site. In 1849 John H. Day and Charles Sevier were added to the committee, and in April of that year a 100-acre tract, lying about two miles north of Jackson, was purchased of Samuel Lancaster, for the sum of $600. The farm was put under the care of Mr. John Irvin, as superintendent till 1854, when this farm also was ordered sold. The county was without a poor-house till 1866, when a new committee, consisting of Wm. Alexander, Felix Rutherford, John Irvin, Richard Withers, H. H. Hodgson, J. R. Chapell and James Blackmon, were chosen to select a new site for a poor-house. This committee did not succeed in making a purchase. In January A. S. Rodgers, with A. R. Reid, H. H. Hodgson, R. W. Sims and James Blackmon, as advisory committee, purchased of W. J. Seahorn, a body of 297 acres, for the sum of $3,600 in county warrants. This embraced a farm of good land, and lies about eleven miles southeast of Jackson. James Adams was employed as superintendent, at a salary of $450 for the first year. The poor asylum is managed with comparatively little expense to the county.

The following is a list of the county officers up to the present time: Sheriffs—Thomas Shannon, 1822–26; Mark Christian, 1826–30, resigned in February, and was succeeded by Daniel Madden; Daniel Madden, 1830–34; Nathaniel Deberry, 1834–38; James McDonald, 1838–40; G. H. Kyle, 1838–42; J. S. Lyon, 1842–44; J. L. McClellan, 1844–46; J. C. Stewart, 1846–48; J. R. Jelks, 1848–54; J. J. Brooks, 1854–60; J. R. Woodfork, 1860–62; G. S. Perkins, 1865–70; R. M. May, 1870–78; W. F. Blackard, 1878–84; B. R. Person, 1884–86, incumbent. County court clerk—Roderick McIver, 1822–34; Thomas W. Gamewell, 1834–56; P. C. McCowat, 1856–72; W. H. Parkham, 1872–76; S. D. Barrett, 1876–78; E. A. Clark, 1878–86; F. W. Adamson, 1886, incumbent.

Circuit clerks—Beverly Randolph, 1822; resigned in October, and was succeeded by Wm. Harris; Wm. Harris, 1822–36; Andrew Guthrie, 1836–52; J. L. Brown, 1852–56; S. W. Boon, 1856–74; R. A. Sneed, 1874–82; W. L. Utley, 1882–86; B. J. Howard, 1886, incumbent. Register—John T. Porter, 1822; J. D. McClellan, 1836–48; W. B. Gates, 1848–56; W. G. Cockrill, 1856–62; J. R. Chappell, 1865–70; Henry McCutchen, 1870–75; W. H. Bruton, 1875–76; J. M. Hardage, 1876–82; J. W. Wallace, 1882–86: incumbent. Clerks and master—Thomas Clark, 1846–73; D. M. Wisdom, 1873–82; M. L. Vesey, 1882–84; R. B. Hurt, 1884, incumbent. Judges—Joshua Haskell, 1822–40; John Read, 1840–62; G. W. Reeves, 1865; W. P. Bond, 1866–70; Gideon B. Black, 1870–76; H. W. McCorry, 1876–82; T. C. Muse, 1882–86; L. S. Woods, 1886, incumbent. Chancellors—Andrew McCampbell, 1846–48; Calvin Jones, 1848–59; John Read, 1859–62 (July, Fourth District); J. W. Harris, 1865–69; T. C. Muse, 1869–70; James Fentress, 1870–75; H. W. McCorry, 1875–82; T. C. Muse, 1880–86; A. G. Hawkins, 1886, incumbent.

The city of Jackson was founded by an act of the General Assembly, passed in 1821–22, entitled an "act to establish a seat of justice for Henry, Carroll, Henderson and Madison Counties." The act called for fifty acres of land, to be deeded to the commissioners. The commissioners chosen by the Legislature were Sterling Brewer and James Fentress. The places had in view for the seat of justice, as elsewhere stated, were Alexandria, Golden's Station and Jackson. The larger portion of the settlers at that time were living at Cotton Grove and vicinity, and as Jackson was a nearer point to them than either of the others, it was looked upon as the more suitable or desirable site for the seat of justice; hence it was chosen. The land to be obtained was to be by donation, or purchase on the most favorable terms. The thirty acres of the original plat of Jackson, lying east of Market Street, was obtained from John McNairy, Joseph Phillips and Wm. E. Butler, attorney, in fact, for the three, on April 9, 1822. Said thirty acres was a part of entry No. 13, for 500 acres owned by said parties. The conditions of the deed were that the lands were to be donated to said commissioners, Brewer and Fentress, but a lot of his own choice was to be reserved by each of the owners in the sale of town lots. Nineteen acres and a portion lying west of Market Street were purchased of David Shannon at $10 per acre, and a choice lot reserved. The last named property was a part of entry No 2, for 170 acres, made by Thomas Shannon, father of David Shannon. The corporate limits of Jackson have been extended fifty acres from time to time, as its growth required. In 1860 it embraced one square mile;

now it embraces two miles square, or four square miles, or 2,560 acres.

The commissioners for the sale of lots consisted of Stokeley D. Hays, Bartholomew G. Stewart, David Horton, James Trousdale, Herndon Haralson, Vincent Haralson, Wm. E. Butler, Robert Hughes and Adam Huntsman, of which committee Herndon Haralson was chosen chairman. The sale of lots did not begin till July 4, 1822, when it continued from time to time as opportunity and necessity required. The commissioners were appointed from time to time as vacancies occurred. They were allowed $4 per day for their services at the first sales, the time charge ranging from seven to eighteen days. Said funds were to be taken out of the moneys arising from the sale of lots. To add spirit to the bidding the county court allowed Joseph Lynn $20 for spirits furnished at the sale. The first purchasers of lots were George Todd, who bought Lot 75; Herndon Haralson, Lot 34; Mark Fisher, Lot 39; Duncan McIver, Lots 32 and 34; Wm. Braden, Lot 63; James McKnight and Wilson McClellan, Lot 48; Vincent Haralson, Lot 16; David Horton, J. H. Ball and Isaac Curry, Lot 24; Wm. Espy, Lots 28 and 59, also a part in 24; A. B. Bradford, Lots 6½ and 25; W. L. Flenen, Lots 45 and 25; James Burns and James K. Polk, Lots 7, 27 and 29, the aggregate cost of the three being $582; Ivy and Breekly, Lot 11; S. F. Gray, Lot 82 and a part of 39; S. C. Crafton, Lot 80; Roderick McIver, Lot 44; and Mr. Legget, Lot 39. This embraces all the lots sold the first year.

Wm. H. Doak was perhaps the first settler within the limits of Jackson, as he raised a crop of corn about where the Public Square now is in 1821. A brother of Mr. Lanty died in Jackson in 1822. This was doubtless the first death within the city limits. Wm. H. soon after moved to the vicinity of Spring Creek, in the northeast part of the county. Jesse Russell, now in his eighty-third year, arrived in Jackson on January 1, 1822, and was married soon after by Squire Taylor. Jesse Russell at first settled on the lot just east of the Episcopal Church. Dr. John F. Brown, an eminent physician, settled in Jackson in 1823. His son, Mr. John Brown, a prominent citizen and lawyer, was born in Jackson in 1824, and still resides in his native city. He is the oldest native resident. Samuel Swan, who kept a small grocery, was the father of the first female child, a daughter, born in Jackson. Dr Wm. E. Butler settled just near the big spring where the water-works now stand. He soon after moved into town and built the large brick residence just east of the institute building, and north of Col. Chester's residence. Dr. Butler was for a long time identified with the business interests of Jackson. He was agent of the old State Bank before the establishment of the Union Bank and Bank of the State of Tennessee.

Stokely D. Hays settled in Jackson in 1822. He was a prominent attorney and a brother-in-law of Dr. Butler. Mrs. Col. Robert Hays, who lived in Jackson at this time, was a sister of Mrs. Gen. Jackson. Gen. Wm. Arnold was for a long time connected with the settlement of the Robinson colony of Americans in Texas; he was also a member of the bar. Col. James Thebold, a brother-in-law of Gen. Arnold, was one of the first inn-keepers in Jackson. Thomas Shannon, who was living in what is now West Jackson at the time of the organization of the county, was sheriff from 1822 to 1826, and was one of the best known citizens. Wm. Armor was one of the most prominent merchants of Jackson in her early history. He was senior member of the firm of Armor, Lake & Co. This firm did an extensive business till it went down in the financial crash of 1838-39. The business house of Armor, Lake & Co. stood where the extensive establishment of Robinson & Botts now stands. James Elrod and H. Harton were extensive business men of Jackson who began business about 1824. They erected a frame business house where Dr. Neeley's drug store now stands. James Elrod was the first to issue ticket notes to circulate as bank notes. Daniel Madden was sheriff of the county from 1830 to 1834; he was beaten for the same office by Thomas Shannon, in 1824, by only two votes. John H. Ball was an inn-keeper, and at one time a blacksmith. He was a successful business man and afterward moved to Somerville. Ball was succeeded in the tavern business by Thomas Winn. Alexander B. Bradford was chosen solicitor-general at the organization, and continued in that office till 1836. Joseph H. Talbot and Alfred Murray were well known lawyers and began practice before the Jackson bar about the time of its formation. Charles Sevier lived here at the time of the organization of the county; he was a hatter by trade. He was a near relative of Gov. John Sevier—"Nollichucky Jack." He afterward moved south of Fork Deer River and settled on an occupant grant. Samuel Taylor was the first postmaster of Jackson. He was also a justice of the peace. Col. R. I. Chester came to Jackson in 1823. His name has been almost a household word throughout the county. He has not only passed his four score and ten, but four score four and ten and bids fair to see the coming of the next century. Dr. Bedford and Dr. Winn were two eminent physicians and were contemporaneous with Dr. John T. Brown. Herndon Haralson was one of the justices in the organization of the county and was a well known citizen. Wm. Stoddert was one of Jackson's first and most distinguished lawyers. James Caruthers, father of Stoddert Caruthers, was one of the most distinguished men of West Tennessee. Andrew L. Martin was prominent before the bar of Jackson in its early history, but afterward moved to Holly Springs. Alexander Patton is claimed to have kept the first store in Jackson. He did an extensive business and was a partner for a time with Wm. E. Butler. J. W. Campbell became cashier of the branch of the Union Bank that was established at Jackson, in 1832–33, and was afterward United States minister to Russia. Pleasant N. Miller was an excellent lawyer and was long and favorably known. He afterward moved to Holly Springs, Miss. In addition to these there was the family of the Nelsons and the Hicks. These embraced all, with few exceptions, who were living in Jackson at the beginning of 1824. Robert Brown came to Jackson in 1826 and is still living in it. Others have resided in Jackson between sixty and seventy years. Hon. R. J. Hays, son of Stokely D. Hays, came to Jackson with his parents, where he has since resided. He is a member of the bar and was the first mayor of Jackson; he is one of the survivors of the Mexican war.

Nearly all business houses from 1820 to 1850 were general stores. Dry goods, groceries, hardware, etc., were all kept by each merchant. The leading business men from 1820 to 1840 were Armor & Lake, Armor, Lake & Co., James Patton, Patton & Taylor, David Armor and James Elrod. The financial crash of 1838–39 ruined the greater number of these, some of whom never recovered. From 1840 to 1860, when business was stopped by the war, the business was done principally by James Elrod, G. N. Harris, H. J. Morrell, J. Miller, Person & Christian, B. Mitchell, T. & J. Collins, Glass & Son. Since 1865 to the present, the leading business houses are: Dry goods, Robinson & Botts, F. E. Bond, W. Holland, J. R. Withers, M. Tuchfeld, Sam Weingarten & Co., Williams & Perry, D. L. Murrell, J. Hoffman, J. Zimmerman, Marks & Bro. and F. Mayo; groceries, A. D. Dugger, G. H. Ramsey & Co., Burkett & Fletcher, Duke & Wisdom, J. P. Hendrix, Hill & Stedman, H. Baum, W. R. Griffith, J. N. Rosser, E. Felsenthal, M. M. Hammond and S. F. Gilkin; drug stores, M. S. Neely, Harris & Ward, M. P. McChesney, R. M. Hamner, Cooper & Co.; jewelers, E. H. Kelly, D. M. Hughes; furniture, R. E. Hopper, W. Bensinger & Son, Job Umphlett and W. D. Robinson; stoves, hardware—R. H. Anderson & Son, G. C. Anderson, J. M. Reavis, Bates & Gorman; books, J. G. Cisco, J. M. Trotter; hats and caps, W. F. Alexander; clothing, Robinson & Botts, Henry Levi; wagon and buggies, Landis & Bro., J. H. Hirsch; merchant tailor, T. Murphy, Harry Meyer; cotton brokers, Dupree, Gates & Co., Capt. McCutchen, R. & J. Blackmon, Haley & Bro.

Jackson is in a very healthful condition financially, notwithstanding her last improvements in streets, gas lights, water-works, etc. The receipts for taxes have been gradual, and show a rapid increase in wealth and population. In 1858 the receipts were $4,462; in 1869, $10,058, and in 1882 (the highest) they were $36,861. The city has a floating debt of only about $15,000, and the water-works bonds of $100,000. The first is an insignificant sum and the latter is met by water privileges as fast as they become due. City bonds are readily taken at par. March 20, 1882, the city purchased of the Fire Extinguisher Manufacturing Company, of Chicago, one Champion Chemical Fire Extinguisher, one hand water engine, hose, reel hooks and ladder and other apparatus. The whole cost $2,000 less $37 off for cash and $800 due in twelve months' time, with interest at 6 per cent until paid.

In 1883 the city decided, by popular vote, to issue $100,000 in bonds for the purpose of building water-works. Estimates of costs had been made by E. L. Cook, of Toledo, Ohio. The bonds were issued in style of $2,000 and $8,000 each, to be floated at par, drawing 5 per cent interest. One of each kind was to be due in 1894, one in 1896 and so on till 1913, when the last ones were to be due. The final estimate by item, including the civil engineer, was $99,372.26. The works are of the finest workmanship, and the water, which is remarkably pure, is obtained from a system of wells and a reservoir near the city. The city now has over six miles of mains, and owns its excellent system of works. The water can be thrown over the highest buildings in the city in large streams. It is by direct pressure from the engines. The water privileges will in a few years fully meet the expense of the investment. The city made a very fortunate venture.

Jackson continued under the government of the town board, which was a creature of the county court, till its incorporation, on December 16, 1845. An election was held by Sheriff Lyon to choose town officers. These officers held their first meeting on December 25, 1845. R. J. Hays was chosen mayor, which position he held till his resignation in 1846 to go to the Mexican war. The act incorporating the city legalized all acts of the town commissioners. Jackson was reincorporated on March 3, 1854, with greater powers, with the usual power granted to a mayor and board of aldermen. The minute book shows the usual fines for petty offense; among them are "fighting," "attempting to fight," "wanting to fight," "lewdness," "riding on the sidewalk," "contempt," "swearing," "gaming," "sneezing," "hallooing," etc. The following is a list of the mayors, recorders and town constables or city marshals as far as can be ascertained:

1845, R. J. Hays, mayor. 1846, R. J. Hays and J. L. H. Tomlin, mayor. 1854, Alexander Jackson, mayor; J. C. Green, recorder. 1855,

Alexander Jackson, mayor; J. C. Green, recorder. 1856, R. J. Hays, mayor; A. W. Campbell, recorder; J. W. Norwood, city marshal. 1857, S. Cypert, mayor; J. C. Green, recorder; J. W. Norwood, city marshal. 1858, R. J. Hays, mayor; J. C. Green, recorder; J. W. Norwood, city marshal. 1859, Wm. Alexander, mayor; A. W. Campbell, recorder; J. J. McAlexander, city marshal. 1860, J. H. Harper, mayor; B. R. Campbell, recorder; J. J. McAlexander, city marshal. 1861, P. D. W. Conger, mayor; B. R. Campbell, recorder; J. J. McAlexander, city marshal. 1862, R. J. Mason, mayor; B. R. Campbell, recorder; H. H. Whiteside, city marshal. 1865, Dr. G. Adamson, mayor; J. H. Harper, recorder; J. J. McAlexander, city marshal. 1866, Wm. Alexander, mayor; J. H. Harper, recorder; J. J. McAlexander, city marshal. 1867, Wm. Alexander, mayor; J. H. Harper, recorder; J. C. Cook, city marshal. 1868, J. J. McAlexander, mayor; B. R. Person, recorder; J. H. Clark, city marshal. 1869, Wm. Alexander, mayor; B. R. Person, recorder; Wm. F. McCabe, city marshal. 1870, Wm. M. Dunaway, mayor; Robert W. May, recorder; Wm. F. McCabe, city marshal. 1871, P. D. W. Conger, mayor, Robert W. May, recorder; Wm. F. McCabe, city marshal. 1872, Wm. M. Dunaway, mayor; Robert W. May, recorder; Wm. F. McCabe, city marshal. 1873, D. H. King, mayor; Robert W. May, recorder; Wm. F. McCabe, city marshal. 1874, J. A. Arrington, mayor; Robert W. May, recorder; Wm. F. McCabe, city marshal. 1875, D. H. King, mayor; John T. King, recorder; H. C. Anderson, city marshal. 1876, D. H. King, mayor; John T. Stark, recorder; H. C. Anderson, city marshal. 1877, L. E. Talbot, mayor; John T. Stark, recorder; J. D. Marks, city marshal. 1878, W. D. Robinson, mayor; John T. Stark, recorder; J. D. Marks, city marshal. 1879, James O'Conner, mayor; John T. Stark, recorder; J. D. Marks, city marshall. 1880, B. R. Person, mayor (resigned, and was succeeded by W. D. Robinson); John T. Stark, recorder; J. D. Marks, city marshal. 1881, J. M. Sullivan, mayor; John T. Stark, recorder; J. D. Marks, city marshal. 1882, B. L. Rozell, mayor; John T. Stark, recorder; J. D. Marks, city marshal. 1883, Col. John W. Buford, mayor; John T. Stark, recorder; J. D. Marks, city marshal. 1884, Col. John W. Buford, mayor (resigned, succeeded by H. C. Anderson); John T. Stark, recorder; J. D. Marks, city marshal. 1885, W. D. Robinson, mayor; John T. Stark, recorder; J. D. Marks, city marshal. 1886, W. D. Robinson, mayor; John T. Stark, recorder; J. D. Marks, city marshal.

The Jackson Compress Company was incorporated April 3, 1880, by George St. John, John O. White, W. H. Long, B. R. Cameron and Thomas St. John. This company does an extensive business. The Jackson Ice Company was incorporated by Howel E. Jackson, A. W. Campbell, N. S. White, R. A. Allison and J. W. Allison. It was incorporated in 1883, for the purpose of manufacturing ice, mineral water, cider, aerated beverages; to bottle and vend beer and ale; to vend wood, coal, lumber and building material. Capital stock was limited from $20,000 to $40,000. The Jackson Woolen Mills were incorporated in January, 1884, by J. L. Wisdom, H. W. McCorry, S. D. Hays, J. H. Duke, B. R. Harris and W. A. Caldwell. The company manufacture jeans, linseys, blankets, wool rolls and yarns. In January the Telephone Company of Jackson was incorporated by H. W. McCorry, C. G. Bond, D. F. Haney, L. S. Woods and W. T. Logan. The company now has in use over 100 instruments. The Champion Mills were incorporated in June, 1884, by J. L. Wisdom, H. W. McCorry, A. H. Duke and J. J. Rushing. The Sherman Manufacturing Company was incorporated in June, 1884, by Nathan S. Sherman, W. B. Cole, A. E. McGarey, M. F. Murdock and W. A. Caldwell. They manufacture and repair farm implements, engine boilers and saw-mill machinery. The Center City Mills were incorporated for a period of thirty-three years, with the usual power, by P. D. W. Conger, R. B. Hurt, B. A. Hays, James Harrison and N. H. Whitlow. The Jackson Oil Mills were established at Jackson in 1879 and 1880. An amended charter was obtained in April, 1886. The firm consists of J. L. Wisdom, P. J. Murray, H. E. Jackson and A. J. Porter. The officers are J. W. Allison, president, and P. J. Murray, secretary. This is an extensive establishment and manufactures all the various products of the cotton seed, including the "Jackson Fertilizer." The Jackson Milling and Manufacturing Company was chartered in the spring of 1885 by J. H. Duke, J. M. McGathery, S. D. Hays, W. A. Caldwell, W. M. Johns and C. Dancey. Its object was to manufacture flour, meal, barrels, kegs, and to buy and sell grain, seeds, wood, lumber and coal. The Jackson Gas Works were founded in 1868. The company was to be known as the Jackson Gas Light Company, and was composed of J. H. Harper, J. L. Tomlin, Robert Hart, R. I. Chester, J. Beverage, Wm. Alexander and Charles Leatherman. The company now has about sixty lamps, and mains reaching to every part of the city. The Jackson Building & Saving Association was chartered March 22, 1880, by E. S. Mallory, J. W. Allison. J. T. Stark, J. H. Freeman, J. H. Hirsch, Howell E. Jackson, W. P. Robertson, J. T. McCutchen, R. A. Sneed and J. T. Beverage. The present officers are J. H. Hirsch, president; F. W. Adamson, secretary; N. S. White, treasurer; E. S. Mallory, attorney. The semi-annual report, ending April 30, 1886, shows that the association held $175,200 in mortgages on real estate, $3,716.45 in unpaid dues, interest, etc.; $203.95 in office furniture; $490 in real estate, and $3,049.61 cash in the treasury.

The Jackson Free Library Association was incorporated February 1, 1886, by L. J. Brooks, F. M. Smith, D. L. Murrell, E. S. Mallory, G. C. Jones, H. Hawkins, A. P. Bourland, C. A. McCorry, N. Bond, J. G. Cisco and A. J. McGehee.

The first bank in Jackson was simply an agency of the old State Bank, which had its agent in the various cities of the State; Wm. E. Butler was the agent at Jackson. The next was the branch of the Union Bank, which was established here in 1831–32, with J. W. Campbell as cashier. This well known institution continued operations until it was closed by the war. On the resumption of business after the war, a savings bank was established in Jackson; this continued until the organization of the First National Bank. This institution was chartered August 24, 1874; James W. Anderson was chosen president. The directors were J. W. Anderson, Jno. M. Parks. W. K. K. Walsh, Milton T. Brown and W. A. Caldwell. The report of the cashier for October, 1886, shows the bank to have capital stock paid in, $50,000, surplus $15,000; undivided profits, national bank notes outstanding, dividends unpaid, individual deposits, etc., to the total amount of $208,649.85. The present directors of the bank are J. L. Wisdom, president; Hon. Howell E. Jackson, vice-president; W. A. Caldwell, cashier; Chester G. Bond, attorney; John A. Greer, Samuel M. White, assistant cashier; W. A. Caldwell, book-keeper and accountant; H. B. Gilmore, collector. The Second National Bank has just been opened for business (1886); the capital stock is $75,000. The officers are John A. Pitts, president; W. T. Nelson, vice-president; N. S. Moore, cashier. The board of directors are John A. Pitts, W. T. Nelson, Clifton Dancy, C. T. Bates, T. C. Abbott, S. D. Hays, H. H. Swink, L. J. Brooks and M. H. Meeks. The Bank of Madison began operations under charter, in June, 1866, with A. W. Campbell as president, and D. J. Merriwether as cashier. The capital stock was $50,000, at which it still remains. The present officers are N. S. White, president, and J. W. Theus, cashier.

The first newspaper, the Jackson *Gazette*, was issued first on May 29, 1824, by Col. Charles De McLean and Elijah Bigelow, and Ed. Hays. Col. McLean was a native of Virginia, where he was born in 1795, and came to Jackson in 1823–24. The *Gazette* was continued until 1830, when it became the *Southern Statesman*, and was edited by Judge Read and Timothy P. Scurlock. The *Statesman* was merged into the *Truth Teller*, in the fall of 1832, and was edited by James H. McMahon. This was continued by him until 1836, when he left for the Seminole war. The next newspaper venture was the *Telegraph*, a Whig paper, by B. H. Shepherd. This was not a success, and was discontinued after about one year. The next paper was a Democratic paper, by a learned Virginian, named Street. This paper was short-lived, as was a Whig paper published by Henry Swan. The *Jacksonian* was published by Rogers & Acton, in 1844. W. F. Doherty began the publication of a small Democratic paper in 1845–46, but it was soon after suspended. In 1855 J. H. Young started the *Jeffersonian*, but it, too, suspended in 1856. The paper, and it might be said, its editor, passed into the hands of Col. W. W. Gates. The next effort at a Whig paper was by —— Mitchell, in 1841–42, but this suspended in a short time. The *West Tennessee Whig* was established by Col. W. W. Gates, who continued its publication until the office was closed and destroyed by the war. After the war Col. Gates with Don Cameron revived his paper, and continued its publication untill 1870, when it was consolidated with the *Tribune*, which had been started by the Milligan Bros., but edited by Col. D. M. Wisdom. This partnership continued until 1872, when Col. Gates retired.

The Jackson *Sun* was first published in September, 1873, by Conner & Harald, and in 1877 by Gates & Enloe. In 1878 the *Tribune* and *Sun* were consolidated under the name of *Tribune and Sun*, under which name it is still published. It is published by the Tribune and Sun Publishing Company. John W. Gates retired from the firm in 1884. The *Tribune and Sun* is a widely circulated paper, and is edited with very marked ability.

In 1877 Col. W. W. Gates again started in the newspaper business. He again took the name of his old paper, *West Tennessee Whig*, which he edited about one year, when he sold it to William H. Brutin, L. J. Brooks, W. A. Ward and D. L. Balch. In September of that year Mr. Balch retired, and in July. 1883, L. J. Brooks and W. A. Ward became proprietors, Since January, 1885, the paper has been issued as a semi-weekly. It is now the only semi-weekly paper in West Tennessee. It is a twenty-eight column four-page paper, and is owned and managed by L. J. Brooks. The *Whig* is a Democratic paper.

The first number of the *Jackson Dispatch* was issued in October, 1873, by J. J. Worrell, who is its present editor. Notwithstanding the misfortune of two fires, opposition of rivals, the *Dispatch* has to-day a wider circulation than ever before. Its circulation extends throughout West Tennessee, Mississippi, Arkansas and Texas. The *Dispatch* is a conservative Democratic paper. It is strictly a peoples' paper. The *True Baptist* is a new religious journal, which was founded by Rev. Frederick Howard, D. D., in April, 1885. He is its editor, publisher and proprietor. The *True Baptist* is an able exponent of the doctrines of the Missionary Baptist Church. It also gives general news, and discusses the various theological questions and church ethics. *The Forked Deer Blade*, a spicy, breezy, independent Democratic paper, was founded by J. G. Cisco in 1883. The paper is printed on a steam-power press, and has a circulation in thirty States. J. G. Cisco, its editor and proprietor, is an excellent writer.

Jackson Lodge, No. 45, F. & A. M., worked first under a dispensation granted in 1822, but was regularly chartered on October 6, 1823. The charter bears the signature of Andrew Jackson, Grand Master of the State of Tennessee, and Thomas Clayton, D. G. M.; — Cooper, S. G. W.; W. E. Kennedy, J. G. W.; W. Tannehill, G. S. The charter was granted to Robert Murray, Daniel Madding, Austin A. King and others. Of these Robert Murray was made W. M., Daniel Madding S. W., and Austin A. King, J. W. Jackson Lodge erected the present hall owned by the lodge in 1850. It is 40x50 feet inside, and is a brick building two stories high. It is used by all the Masonic bodies.

St. John's Lodge, No. 332, was organized from Jackson Lodge. On October 8, 1867, a charter was granted to St. John's Lodge, No. 332. The grand officers of the State were J. M. Anderson, G. M.; J. W. Paxton, D. S. M.; J. S. Dancer, S. G. W.; J. M. Hughes, J. G. W., and C. A. Fuller, G. S. The first officers of this lodge were J. B. Morris, W. M.; N. H. Whitlow, S. W., and J. A. Metcalf, J. W. It may be here stated that Col. R. I. Chester was made a Mason in May, 1822, the oldest now living in the United States. Jackson Lodge was honored by a visit from Gen. Jackson, in 1825. Clinton Chapter, No. 9, was organized in 1827–28. It was not kept up for a time, and on October 14, 1834, it was transferred to Lexington. It was brought back in 1841–42. At the time of the transfer it contained thirteen members and at the time of the return but three of those were left. The officers of the Grand Chapter at that time were J. H. Thomas, G. H. P.; Thomas H. Moore, D. G. H. P.; Joe H. Talbot, King, and J. Grifford, G. S. The chapter was favored with a visit by James K. Polk, in 1844. Council No. 13, was organized October 15, 1851, on petition of Thomas Morse, Robert Stark, J. B. Chappell, Phillip Thompson, Wm. A. Dunaway, S. J. Jones, H. G. Bledsoe, J. M. McRee and Geo. Tucker. The first officers were Thomas Morse, M. I. G. C. M.; Robt. Stark, D. I. G. M., and J. B. Chappell, P. C. The State officers were J. P. Campbell, M. R. G. M, and J. O. Dashiell, G. R.

Ancient and Accepted Scottish Rite Masonry, John Chester Lodge of Perfection, No. 1, was instituted in Jackson, Tenn., on the 25th of January, 1879, under charter from the Supreme Council of the southern jurisdiction of the United States of America (mother jurisdiction of the world) at Charleston, S. C.—Albert Pike, Thirty-third Washington (D.

C.) Sovereign Grand Commander; by H. H. Neal, Thirty-third Louisville (Ky.) Special Deputy, with B. R. Harris, Thirty-second Venerable Master; M. R. Robertson, Thirty-second Senior Warden; J. M. McGathery, Thirty-second Junior Warden; S. L. Collins, Thirty-second Treasurer; J. C. Smith, Thirty-second Recorder; Isaac Lewis, Thirty-second Orator; W. M. Johns, Thirty-second Senior Expert; R. A. Sneed, Fourteenth Junior Expert; H. P. Farrar, Thirty-second Master of Ceremonies; M. T. Carson, Third-second Captain of Host; B. R. Harris, Thirty-second, is now Venerable Master, and J. C. Smith, Thirty-second, is Recorder.

The charter to Phœnix Lodge, No. 216, B. of U. W., was granted May 10, 1886, to C. A. Chandler, J. W. Stewart, L. W. Barr, J. W. Williams, W. B. Dunn, J. A. Dalton, W. W. Rooker, Jesse Kyle, J. P. Muse, J. Connors, Wm. Pearcey, R. T. Long, E. T. Arnn, R. S. Hill, C. G. Newman, S. J. Gayle, W. Stout, J. W. Stanley and J. W. Swetman. The lodge meets in the I. O. O. F. Hall.

Trimphant Lodge of Jackson, K. H., was granted a charter of the Grand Lodge of K. H., on May 17, 1885. The charter was signed by C. Allen, Wm. Anderson and thirty-six other members; they meet in the I. O. O. F. Hall, on the corner of Lafayette and Main Streets. Madison Lodge, No. 16, I. O. O. F., was chartered April 1, 1846. The charter members were Robt. Stark, W. K. Parton, A. A. Smithrick, N. Hencott, A. F. Gibbs and J. A. Gilbert. The old charter was destroyed by fire and a new one issued October 18, 1882. This is now one of the largest lodges in the city.

The charter of Lancelot Lodge, No. 13, K. of P., was granted by the Grand Lodge February 10, 1874. The charter members were W. F. Alexander, J. T. Botts, Stoddert Caruthers, J. L. Kendrick, H. W. McCorry, Richard Redman, W. P. Robinson, B. S. Spencer and J. T. Stark. The lodge has an elegant room over Dr. Neely's drug store.

Friendly Hand Lodge, No. 201, Locomotive Engineers, was chartered March 2, 1884. The following are the charter members: Wm. Ruffin, Wm. Cook, Wm. Chilton, John Baker, Samuel Lynn, Timothy Cregleton, Jobe Bailey, J. Campbell, Eugene Simms and Thomas Druan. This lodge meets in the room of the K. of P.

Denmark lies about twelve miles southwest of Jackson and contains about 250 inhabitants. It is in the midst of a rich farming community, and was one of the first places settled in the county. The land on which Denmark stands was opened by Thomas Sanders in 1822. Before the war Denmark did considerable business, but the completion and extension of the railroads have to a great extent taken the trade elsewhere. The place was incorporated in 1854 under the style of mayor and alderman of Denmark. Denmark has had a Presbyterian Church since 1833, a Methodist since 1842, a Baptist since 1871, and a Methodist (colored) since 1873. It sustains a good school. The high school was chartered in 1885 by M. Murchison, Anderson Taylor, J. A. Bryant, J. L. Burton, F. E. Bryant and G. W. Day.

Spring Creek Postoffice is thirteen miles northeast of Jackson at the crossing of the Trenton and Lexington road with the Jackson, Spring Creek and Huntington road. This is more a county or neighborhood postoffice than a town. It was, however, incorporated on January 2, 1854. The Cumberland Presbyterian and Masonic Lodge, No. 193, erected a church and lodge room there in 1865. It also contains a Baptist Church and Madison College. Some fine estates lie near Pinson, twelve miles south of Jackson on the Mobile & Ohio Railroad, in District No. 1. It is located on a small stream called Bear Creek. It is a thriving place of about 300 inhabitants. Pinson contains a good school building, a Baptist Church and a Methodist Church and Masonic Hall combined. Pinson is a good shipping point for the southern part of the county.

Medon, comprising about 300 souls, is situated ten miles south of Jackson on the Illinois Central Railroad. It is surrounded by a rich farming community. Medon has a good brick school building and a Masonic Hall. The Medon High School was incorporated in 1881 by W. H. Harrison, J. A. Haynes, J. P. Cobb, Wm. Pope, G. E. McDaniel and John McDaniel. Claybrook, fourteen miles east of Jackson; Carroll Station, six miles north on the Mobile & Ohio Railroad; Norwood, eight miles north on the Illinois Central, and Malesus, four miles south on the same road, are stations, and have postoffices and business houses. There is also a postoffice at Andrews' Chapel, in District No. 7.

The county court for Madison was organized on December 17, 1821. It consisted of the justices appointed by the Legislature, mentioned on organization, and the following constables: George White, John Fare, Elijah Jones and Wm. H. Doak. Alex. B. Bradford appeared and took the several oaths as solicitor-general of the Fourteenth Solicitorial District. The sheriff's first *venire* embraced the following persons: John Montgomery, Henry N. Coulter, Lewis Needham, Martin Lorance, John Hardgrove, Smith Sullivan, James Dollard, Moses Oldham, Francis Taylor, Zachariah Thomas, Wm. Davis, Sam'l Shannon, John Bradberry, Thomas Jones, Wm. L. Parker, Benjamin Jones, David Jernigan, Wm. Espy, Vincent Haralson, James Caldwell, James Harly Raygin, Francis Herron, Nathan Simpson, James Brown and C. C. Collier. The justices were divided into classes so as to hold quarter sessions. Wm. Atchison, Rob H. Dyer, Duncan McIver, A. R. Alexander, Bartholomew G. Stewart and Joseph Lynn were to hold courts in June and December, and John Thomas, Wm. Braden, David Jarnett, James Trousdale, Herndon Haralson and Samuel Taylor in March and September. This court selected Francis Taylor's and Wm. P. Scott's, on Middle Fork; Henry Ruthferford's, Key Corner; J. D. Caruther's and Daniel Ross', on South Fork, and Thomas McNeal's on the south side of Big Hatchie, as the place of holding elections. This court established ferry rates as follows: Each loaded wagon, four horses, $1; three horses, 75 cents; two-horse team and wagon, 50 cents; each man and horse, $6\frac{1}{4}$ cents; loose horse, $2\frac{1}{2}$ cents; each head of cattle, $2\frac{1}{2}$ cents; sheep or hog, 2 cents. The ordinary rates fixed were: Each diet, 25 cents; lodging, $12\frac{1}{2}$ cents; horse-feed all night, $37\frac{1}{2}$ cents; single feed, $18\frac{3}{4}$ cents; half pint of domestic spirits, $12\frac{1}{2}$ cents; foreign spirits, 25 cents. These continued with little variation for many years. The court was confined largely to the approval of officers' bonds, granting the right for mill sites, building bridges, recording stock marks, making allowance for wolfs' scalps, and much other of such matter. On August 10, 1826, was spread upon record a beautiful memorial to Thomas Jefferson and John Adams. The jurisdiction of the county court at Jackson was much more circumscribed than were the county courts in some of the older counties, when the county court was the only court in existence for some time. The first State case was the State against Squire Dawson for petit larceny. He was found guilty, September 18, 1822, but took an appeal to the circuit court. In 1824 there was a succession of slander suits. Henry Pace secured $100 against John Graves; T. M. Dement, $65 against Thomas Boling; and Wm. C. Love, $799 against Jonathan Houston, but he was released by the plaintiff. On September 28, the following entry was made: "Ordered that John Fussell be fined $10 for contempt shown this court for fighting John Montgomery in the court yard, during the sitting of the court, to the great disturbance of the same."

The circuit court of Madison County was established by an act of the General Assembly, passed November 4, 1821, called a court of "Law and Equity for the Eighth Circuit." A commission was issued by Gen. Carroll to Judge Joshua Haskell, on November 14, 1821. The oath was administered to Judge Haskell by John Smith, presiding justice of the court of pleas and quarter sessions of Rutherford County. The court held its first session at Alexander's office, where the county court met; on April 14, 1822. The officers of the court, besides Judge Haskell, were Thomas Shannon, sheriff, and Beverly Randolph, circuit clerk. The first grand jury consisted of Adam R. Alexander, foreman; J. T. Porter, Wm. E. Butler, Duncan McIver, Ezekiel B. McCoy, Wm. L. Davis, W.

C. Love, W. C. Mitchell, Benjamin White, Wm. Doak, Geo. Todd, Roland Chandler and Drury Belter. On the organization of the court, the following attorneys were admitted: J. W. Cocke, Alex B. Bradford, James Jones, Robert Hughes and Archibald C. Hall. Judge Haskell remained on the bench till 1840, when he was succeeded by Judge John Read. Judge Haskell lived at "Haskell Hill," in Jackson, and was a man highly respected for his character, courtly bearing and pleasant manners. He was the father of Wm. Haskell, one of Tennessee's greatest orators. Alex B. Bradford, the first solicitor-general, was a very popular attorney. He moved to Mississippi in 1834. Joseph Talbot, the second solicitor-general, was considered a very able prosecutor, and more than an average lawyer. The first cases in the circuit court were the cases of Wm. Newsom against J. B. Hogg, and Rob H. Dyer and Jonathan Curren against Robert H. Dyer. Both were cases of debt. The first State case was the State against Squire Dawson, on an appeal from the county court, for petit larceny. The decision was to the effect that Dawson should receive twenty lashes on the bare back, well laid on. This occurred on October 22, 1822, and was the first punishment of the kind ordered. The first divorce suits were filed by Patsey Dun against Joseph Dun, and James Ricketts against Jenny, his wife. The former case was stricken from the docket, and the latter granted. In 1823 G. B. Chambers obtained $12\frac{1}{2}$ cents damage against L. D. Waddel in a suit for damage. Fines were inflicted for betting on cards, roulette, "bazoon" and the wheel of fortune. The first case of horse stealing was the case of the State against Adam Lowry, on November 28, 1824. The jury in the case were J. B. Cross, Robert Lowing, H. G. Connally, W. Ray, H. W. James, Wm. Espy, William Nichols, Gabriel Chandler, James A. Edwards and Robert Hasster. This was before the penitentiary law, and the punishment in this case was that Lowry should be taken to the public whipping post, and there receive thirty-nine lashes, be branded upon the brawn of the thumb with "H. T.," should be sent to jail for thirty days, and made to stand in the pillory two hours of every three days out of seven, be rendered infamous, and be made to pay the cost of his prosecution.

The first murder trial began in October, 1826, and ended January 31, 1827, in conviction. The case was the State against Thomas Jameson, for the murder of Francis Sanders. Jameson was an objectionable suitor for the hand of Sanders' daughter. The murder was committed for the purpose of securing the wished for prize. The prisoner was remanded to jail to remain till May 4, 1827, between 10 A. M. and 2 P. M., when he should be taken to a convenient place near Jackson, and there hung by the neck until dead. The execution was duly carried out about two miles from Jackson. A negro was also executed as an accomplice. At the July term of the same year, James Wright, for the killing of West Ratcliff, was convicted of manslaughter and ordered to pay a fine of $25 and the cost of his prosecution, also to be branded on the thumb with the letter "M." The first case to the penitentiary after the passage of the penitentiary law, was William Morgan, convicted of horse stealing. He was convicted January 23, 1834, and sentenced for a term of three years, and was rendered infamous. A motion for a new trial, also a motion for arrest of judgment was overruled. On July 24, 1834, was ended a suit that was well known throughout the State. It was the suit of the State against John A. Murrell, for negro stealing. Whether guilty or not guilty, he was accused of almost every crime known to the criminal calendar. The jurymen in the well known case were Joseph Hogg, Chas. Robertson, J. G. Snodgrass, Henry Tate, Samuel Lancaster, Granderson Spurlock, David Robertson, John Rodgers, David McKnight, A. H. Morrow, Jacob Sneed and James Elrod. Murrell was sentenced to the penitentiary for a term of ten years. He was defended by Milton Brown. All motions for new trial and arrest of judgment were overruled. Elizabeth Murrell, sister of the above was convicted of larceny and sentenced for one year, but was recommended for mercy and received a nominal fine. The attorneys to 1834, in addition to those mentioned already, were John Wyatt, who died in 1824. A committee consisting of J. H. Talbot, Alfred Murray and Adam Huntsman, said he was one of "our brightest ornaments and best brothers." On June 17, 1823, J. S. Allen, Benjamin Gillespie, Hugh W. Dunlop and Andrew McCampbell were admitted to the bar, and June 27, 1824, M. A. McKenzie. These men were only fairly well known to the Jackson bar. Adam Huntsman, one of the ablest statute lawyers Jackson ever had, was a native of Virginia. He moved to Knoxville in early life, where he read law with Judge John Williams. He moved to Monroe County, where he remained till 1824, when he came to Jackson, where he remained till his death on August 23, 1849. The committee that drew up the memorial of his death consisted of Judge John Read, Henry Brown, Samuel McClanahan, A. W. O. Totten, Micajah Bullock and Milton Brown. Adam Huntsman served as State senator, was a member of the constitutional convention of 1834, and a member of Congress. He beat the celebrated Davy Crockett in the last race Crockett ever ran. Huntsman was never beaten for office. Andrew L. Martin began practice in Jackson in 1825 or 1826. He was widely known as a lawyer and politician. He moved to Mississippi between 1840 and 1850. William Stoddert, one of the ablest and best known lawyers of the Jackson bar, began practice in 1822 and continued until his death recently.   Milton Brown first became known to the profession in 1832. He was a law partner of Wm. Stoddert, and by many was considered the ablest man ever before the Jackson courts.   Samuel McClanahan was an eminent lawyer, and began practice at Jackson about 1834.   Other attorneys were William Anderson, Austin King, James Jones, Daniel Thomas, T. A. Warren, A. C. Hall, D. W. Maury, Robert Hughes, Wm. Arnold, John W. Cocke, W. B. Miller, P. M. Miller, Stokely D. Hays, Wm. Arnold and Robert Hodge.

Judge John Read received his commission as circuit judge in 1840, and held that position till the courts were closed by the war in 1862. Judge Read was a man of a clear judicial mind, firm, upright and honest. He was plain in his dress, but affable in manner.   About the time of Judge Read's coming upon the stage there came a class of eminent lawyers.   Alex B. Bradford was succeeded as attorney-general, for the time being, by Henry W. McCorry in 1836, and he by Wm. N. Porter in 1837, and he by Wm. B. Miller, till 1840, who moved away, and Joseph H. Talbot received his commission from Gov. Polk, on April 23, 1840.   Timothy P. Scurlock became attorney-general in 1846, and was succeeded by J. R. Stephens in November, 1850.

The third legal hanging in Madison occurred about 1838.   It was a man named Reiley, for the murder of a man named Willis.   The killing occurred about ten miles east of Jackson, and the execution followed in due time and form.   The court of 1838 sent S. R. Smith and Burwell Clark each to the penitentiary for three years, for forgery, B. W. H. Medares three years for larceny.   A very exciting suit, in which money, talent and social influence were involved, was the suit of J. L. Tarbutton against W. M. Price, for the seduction of his daughter.   The case was begun in April, 1837.   The best legal talent was employed in the suit. It was taken to Haywood County, where it was compromised.   The plaintiff recovered $1,000 and costs.   The suit of Sanders vs. Stores in a case of ejectment, lasted from 1840 to 1848; also the suit of Cole vs. Sanders.   The case grew out of the purchase of a negro by the former from the latter.   It was alleged that Sanders had sold the plaintiff an unsound negro.   The case lasted from 1844 to 1848.   In May, 1859, A. Williams was found guilty of "rape" and was sentenced to the penitentiary for twenty-one years.   The last court before the war was held in May, 1861, with Judge Read presiding.   The jury summoned consisted of J. W. Sharp, A. B. Goodwin, B. Withers, Thomas Campbell, W. H. Brown, F. G. Gibbs, J. B. Cole, J. P. Thomas, J. M. Greer, W. M. Tidwell and Henry Glen. In 1849, August 23, Adam Huntsman, before mentioned, died.   A committee consisting of Henry Brown, Judge John Read, Samuel McClanahan, A. W. O. Totten, Micajah Bullock and Melton Brown drew up suitable memorials. David Reid died August 27, 1858. A memorial of his death was also spread upon record. The courts were reopened after the war by Geo. W. Reeves as judge; G. G. Perkins, sheriff, and Sion W. Boon, on November 20, 1865. In 1866 Wm. R. Bond received his commission as judge, and Wm. F. Tally, attorney-general.

Numerous suits followed soon after the war, some of which sprang from bitterness and were engendered by the war. Happily these difficulties soon passed away. On April 25, 1874, Milton McLoed shot and killed Thaddeus Pope. McLoed was arrested, tried, convicted, and on January 7, 1876, was executed before an immense throng. The stoicism manifested by the defendant throughout the entire proceedings was remarkable. On July 13, 1876, Millard Filmore Wilson (colored) murdered Capt. Newton C. Perkins, and on the anniversary of his crime was executed. Judge Milton Brown died in October, 1882. He was born in Lebanon, Ohio, in 1804, and came to Jackson some time after the organization, and shone like a meteor for more than half a century. His name vividly calls up recollections of Martin Huntsman, Read, Haskell, Caruthers, McClanahan, Totten, Scurlock, Stephens, Bullock, Miller and many others. The bar of Jackson has long been represented by an eminent class of attorneys. Being as it is, a central point for West Tennessee, a vast amount of litigation has been had before it. Fifty trials for murder seem large, yet it is not, compared with other portions of the country, and the area embraced in its range. No morbid desire induced this statement, but it simply stands as a truth. The criminality of these offenses ranges from the greatest to the most trivial.

From the rule book appears the first suit from the Madison County Chancery Court in 1825. It was a suit of John Henderson, James Caldwell and Wm. Miller against John Overton. The court was then held at Huntingdon, and there appear the depositions of James Mallory, Andrew Jackson and Samuel B. Overton. The first court in Jackson was held May 7, 1846, before Andrew McCampbell, chancellor for the western division, at which time Thomas Clark was appointed clerk and master. Case No. 1 was the suit of Timothy P. Jones against the Planters' Bank for ejectment. It was gained by Jones, and appealed to the supreme court by the defendant. In July, 1848, Calvin Jones became chancellor. The first attorneys' names entered before the chancery court were Gen. Gibbs, R. J. Hays and Geo. W. Bond. In 1865 this court was reorganized by J. W. Harris. The attorneys entering their names at that time were Samuel McClanahan, Henry Brown, W. H. Stephens,

J. H. Tomlin and J. R. Stephens. In 1867 Hon. T. C. Muse became chancellor, and in 1870 James Fentress, with D. N. Wisdom as chancellor and master. The Jackson bar is now represented by McCorry & Bond, Pitts, Hays & Meeks, Bullock & Anderson, R. J. Hays, Caruthers & Mallory, Brown & Herron, J. L. Brown, A. W. Campbell, T. C. Muse, J. B. Robertson, J. L. Lewis, —— Williams, E. G. O'Conner, J. W. Bryant, Tomlin & Haynes.

In the war of 1812 the Third and Fourth Tennessee regiments were raised in East Tennessee. The troops rendezvoused in Rhea County to embark for New Orleans. The order, however, was countermanded, and they were sent direct to Mobile. The Third Regiment was commanded by Col. Thomas Booth, with Wm. Armstrong as adjutant and John Sutherland as quartermaster. The Fourth Regiment was commanded by Samuel Bayless, as colonel; —— Hill, lieutenant-colonel; W. C. Roadman, major; Wm. Bayless, adjutant; Dr. A. Nelson, regimental surgeon, and R. I. Chester, of Jackson, as quartermaster. The men were marched direct to Mobile, where they remained till the news of peace was received. Col. Chester was present when the nine militia-men were shot by order of the court martial called by Gen. Jackson. The men were tried for desertion, mutiny and sedition. The men were led to the place of execution and fifty-four shots were fired at them, and all fell dead, except one, who was severely wounded. He begged for pardon, which was granted, but what the executioners failed to do was accomplished by an ignorant surgeon by bleeding.

In 1836, among the many companies tendering their services, the Madison Grays were accepted. This was organized as a political company, but its services were tendered and accepted by the governor. This was Company B, and its officers were Jesse McMahan, captain; Wise K. Cook, first lieutenant, and Wm. O. Butler, second lieutenant. The company was assigned to the regiment of Col. A. B. Bradford. From Lexington the company went to Fayetteville, the place of rendezvous; thence direct to Montgomery, Ala. Soon after a treaty was made with the Creeks, when the men proceeded to Tallahassee; thence to the Withlacoochee, where a battle was fought with Osceola and Jumper. The men remained in Florida till their term of service (six months) had expired, when they shipped from Tampa Bay to New Orleans, when they were mustered out, and returned home by way of the Mississippi River to Memphis; thence by stage home. The company left home June 25, 1836, and returned January 24, 1837. The only losses by battle were Sergt. Beard, killed, and S. Hays, wounded. It is believed that the only living representatives of the company are Liberty Weir, of Jackson, and Richard Bradford, of Lake County.

On the call of the President for volunteers for the Mexican war, by an act of Congress of May 13, 1846, many were offered, but, indeed, few were chosen. Company F, called Capt. Jones' company, was enrolled at Jackson in May, 1846, and mustered at Memphis on June 4, 1846, by Gen. L. F. Coe. The following is the muster roll of the company, as it appeared April 4, 1847: Timothy Jones, captain; Richard J. Hays, second lieutenant; Alex P. Green, third lieutenant; John R. McClanahan and Horace G. Bledsoe, sergeants; John Thompson, John J. Anderson and James E. Whyte, corporals; William L. Anderson, drummer. Privates: Tyler Anderson, Wm. Browning, Benj. F. Bledsoe, Thomas Boyd, Joe A. Burns, John Burns, Jason H. Clowd, Eli Chandler, Wm. W. Dickerson, L. W. Fussell, Ben F. Gourley, Robt. Faltom, E. B. W. Hobbs, J. Hollingsworth, Robt. Houston, Christopher Johnson, Wm. W. Jones, Wm. G. Mathews, Leander D. Miller, Nathan Miller, I. H. Marks, Wm. Nicks, K. B. Pledger, Everett Pearcy, Samuel Smith, John Stuart, John Swan, John Wright, Alonzo L. Whyte, Solomon Whitlow, Geo. E. Willy, Benj. Williams, John Wagnon and John Woodel. The following were discharged for wounds or disability, at Camargo, Tampico or Vera Cruz: J. B. Freeman, Alex Henderson, Samuel Lyon, E. B. Donelson, C. T. Knight, Wm. A. Day, Hiram Anderson, E. A. Clark, J. C. Cochran, J. B. Cross, Daniel Depriest, Joel Lewis, Geo. W. Lyon, Harris Rhodes, J. F. L. Sevier, Hiram Tomlin and A. Williams. The following were killed in battle, died of wounds, or of sickness: Wyley Pope Hale, Willis Fleming, Thomas Griffins, Robt. Kernan, Ira Martin, Ephraim Price, Geo. A. Smith, Wm. O. Stribbling, Alex Tyner and John Yancy. Of these, Fleming, Griffins, Kernan, Price and Stribbling were killed at Cerro Gordo, April 18, 1847; Hale and Smith were mortally wounded at the same engagement; Martin and Yancy died of disease at Camargo, and Tyner at Metamoras. Capt. Jones' company belonged to the Second Regiment, Tennessee Volunteers, First Brigade. The regimental officers were Wm. T. Haskell, colonel; C. S. Cummings, lieutenant-colonel. The company was an old political organization, and its services were tendered and accepted. The company was known as the "Avengers." The following are believed to be the only survivors of the company: R. J. Hays, H. G. Bledsoe, Everett Pearcy, E. A. Clark, Samuel Smith and James Cole. [For a history of the regiment, see State History in this volume].

On the outbreak of the civil war there was a remarkable unanimity for the South. The first company to tender its aid to the Confederacy was the Southern Guards. After a temporary organization, this, with five other companies, became the major part of the Sixth Tennessee.

Each of these six companies numbered at first fully 150 men. The regimental officers of the Sixth were W. H. Stephens, colonel; T. P. Jones, lieutenant-colonel; Geo. C. Porter, major; R. R. Deshiell, surgeon; J. S. Turner, assistant-surgeon. The officers of the Southern Guards, Company H, were W. C. Penn, captain; Alex. Brown, first lieutenant; John McDonald, second lieutenant; George Taylor, third lieutenant. The Jackson Grays, Company G, as well as the Southern Guards, were made up mainly in and around Jackson. The commissioned officers of G were A. B. Freeman, captain; Isaac Jackson, first lieutenant; James Elrod, second lieutenant; B. F. Bond, third lieutenant. Company K was recruited in the vicinity of Denmark, and was called the "Danes." Their commissioned officers were John Ingram, captain; F. W. Campbell, first lieutenant; Thomas Rice, second lieutenant; James Walker, third lieutenant. The "Madison Invincibles," from Medon and vicinity, were commanded by Westbrook Freeland, captain; Rev. G. L. Winchester, first lieutenant; Thomas Lacey, second lieutenant; R. A. Mays, third lieutenant. Company E, McClanahan Guards, were commanded by J. M. Wollard, captain; J. J. Anderson, first lieutenant; Henry Hill, second lieutenant; J. Fussell, third lieutenant. The "Gadsden Spartans" were commanded by Capt. Collinsworth; Ed. Smith, third lieutenant. Later in the service, after the ranks became depleted, the Sixth was consolidated with the Ninth; Capt. Robert Ford's company of recruits was also added. The other officers of Ford's company were J. D. Bond, first lieutenant; G. Smith, second lieutenant; Lum Sharp, third lieutenant. [See State history for sketch of this regiment.]

The Jeff Davis Guards, Company C, of the Thirty-eighth, was raised and commanded by Job Umphlett, captain. The other commissioned officers were A. B. March, first lieutenant; J. D. Thompson, second lieutenant; W. C. Robinson, third lieutenant. The company originally was composed of seventy-two men.

The Thirty-third Regiment was commanded by Gen. A. W. Campbell, of Jackson. It contained one company from Madison.

Company B, of the Fourteenth Regiment Cavalry, was from Madison County. This company was commanded by Z. Vass, captain; Robt. Stribbling, first lieutenant; B. Halton, second lieutenant; H. H. Swink, third lieutenant. The regimental officers were J. J. Neeley, colonel; Rolla White, lieutenant-colonel; Thomas Thurman, major. The regiment was mustered into the service July 10, 1863, at Gun's Church, Miss. The regiment was with Forrest the greater part of the time. It operated in Mississippi; was with Hood in his disastrous raid upon Nashville, and fell back with the army through Franklin Spring Hill, Columbia, Pulaski, Bainbridge and to Rienzi, where the men were furloughed home ten days. They again assembled at West Point, and passed to Selma (Ala.), Tuscaloosa, and were surrendered at Gainesville.

The Fifty-first Regiment was raised in December, 1861. It was composed of eight companies, four of which were from Madison County. This was commanded by Capts. Hudson, Clark, Elder and Murchison, respectively. The regimental officers were —— Browder, colonel; John Chester, lieutenant-colonel, and E. A. Clark, major. After the reorganization this regiment was consolidated with the Fifty-second. A full history of this regiment is given in the State work.

The county court acted promptly in voting aid to soldiers, and supplies for families of the indigent. In May, 1861, the entire county was organized into militia companies, and their officers appointed, there being altogether eighteen companies. Old guns were tendered for arms. October 7, 1861, J. H. Harper was allowed $140, fourteen pairs of bullet molds, and on April 7, 1862, the county court made a unanimous tender to Gen. Beauregard of the court house bell. In April, 1862, county script was issued to aid soldiers' families. Of this over $7,000 was paid out, and the city of Jackson, in April, 1861, issued bonds to the amount of $5,000, to be used by the committee of safety in procuring arms and ammunition. In a short time $10,000 more was placed at the disposal of the committee.

The Madison Male Academy was chartered by the Legislature in 1834. The trustees were James Caruthers, Milton Brown, Wm. Armor, John W. Campbell, Joshua Haskell, Andrew L. Martin, Wm. E. Butler, J. H. Talbot, J. B. Creighton, D. A. Street and W. A. Stephens. A lot was purchased, known as the Marshall or Hurt property, and a brick building erected thereon by private subscription. The school was managed as an academy till 1843-44, when authority was given for a collegiate school. The trustees named for the West Tennessee College were James Caruthers, John W. Campbell, W. H. Stephens, Milton Brown, Robt. Fenner, M. Cartmell, Alexander Jackson, J. L. Talbot, Sam'l Lancaster, A. W. Campbell, together with Samuel McClanahan, Geo. Snyder, A. W. O. Totten and James Vaulx. The name of the institution was changed, but the trustees were the same and new buildings were added on the same grounds. In 1844 James Caruther exchanged the forty-six acres of ground where the university now stands for the old property and $3,000 in money, the title to be confirmed on payment of same. This land was formerly owned by A. L. Martin, and adjoined the 500-acre tract of McNairy, Butler & Phillips. The title was confirmed January 26, 1855. Before the cession of the Territory of Tennessee by North Carolina to the United States Government, that State reserved military land warrants varying in size from 320 acres to 5,000 acres for her continental soldiers and 100,000 acres for a college in East Tennessee and one in West Tennessee, then embracing both Middle and West Tennessee; 100.000 acres for academies, also one section out of each congressional township for common schools. The land warrants were very difficult claims to adjudicate, as the surveys were very unsatisfactory. In 1806 Congress made the State of Tennessee its agent to carry out its part of the cession act. In 1845-46 Congress was memorialized by the Legislature of Tennessee, when it not only gave up all claims to public lands in Tennessee, but donated $40,000 of the surplus from the sale of lands to the West Tennessee College. The school was thus managed by the trustees till 1874, when the trustees, seeing that the college was only receiving local patronage, and feeling the need of more endowment, that its usefulness might be extended, proposed to the Baptist Church of Tennessee that its buildings, lands, etc., should be given for the use of the faculty of the Southwestern University, then located at Murfreesboro, on condition that the church should raise $300,000 as an additional endowment within ten years. This was afterward modified to $100,000. The faculty of the Southwestern Baptist University opened the academic department in the fall of 1874, since which time it has been in successful operation. The university has held regular commencement exercises since 1876. The number of graduates have varied from one to six. The medical department, which is located at Memphis, was added in 1880. The literary department, which embraces the usual course of such institutions, is under the direction of George W. Jarmen, LL. D., assisted by a corps of thorough and experienced teachers. The university has for support about $50,000 in grounds and buildings, $55,000 in productive funds, $40.000, which is the Government donation and is held in Tennessee bonds, and $15,000 in private donations. In addition the university has about $15,000 of non-productive funds. The remaining source of income is in tuition charged. As soon as the $100,000 endowment is raised, which will doubtless be done soon, it is proposed to erect additional buildings and add other improvements necessary.

The Memphis Conference Female Institute was founded and chartered in 1843, at Jackson. As its name indicates, it is strictly a female school under control of the Methodist Church South. This institution is in the forty-third year of its existence. It employs a faculty of thirteen regular instructors. To the institute twenty-seven commencement sermons have been preached, and twenty-eight annual addresses have been delivered. The first building proved to be inadequate for the demands and in 1855 it was greatly enlarged. The institute has grown in popularity and usefulness notwithstanding opposition and adverse circumstances, until it now ranks among the best in the State. In 1885 the east wing was erected, containing a large dining hall and twelve additional boarding rooms. The main building (four stories high) contains the president's office, family rooms, and seventeen boarding rooms. The west wing contains the chapel, music department, art department, reading room, library of 4,000 volumes, and recitation rooms.

The buildings are of brick and are all under one roof. The grounds are five acres in extent and are tastefully laid in walks, and ornamented with flowers and shaded with trees. About 500 young ladies have graduated from the institute and gone into fields of usefulness. The attendance numbers about 200. The institute, under control of Dr. Jones since its inception, is carried on with singular economy, and is intended to bring out the higher moral and intellectual qualities of the mind.

The Public Schools of Jackson were organized under an amended act of 1873, which was passed in 1881. An ordinance was passed in 1879, under the act of 1873 creating the Jackson City graded schools. The board of education consisted of W. P. Robertson, E. S. Mallory, James O'Conner and J. H. Hirsch, with J. C. Brooks as superintendent with eight assistants. The following tabulated statements show the progress of the schools and other items.

YEAR.	Scholastic Population.	Enrollment.	Attendance.	Number of Teachers.	Time in Days.	Running Expense.	Cost of School.	Value of Property.	Cents per Pupil.
1879–80...............	......	......	457	9	190	$4,000	$5,300	No B'ld'gs. $	86
1880–81...............	1,700	1,017	659	13	180	5,800	7,800	....	97
1881–82...............	1,786	1,008	681	14	180	6,600	8,500	....	1 00
1882–83*..............	......	......	......	15	180	....	....	....	....
1883–84...............	1,786	1,061	691	15	180	6,152	9,626	$6,172	1 00
1884–85...............	1,992	1,038	751	17	180	7,795	8,994	8,200	1 14
1885–86...............	1,992	1,214	957	19	180	9,778	10,354	10,955	1 12

The above is rather a remarkable showing when it is considered that the schools are now in the eighth year of their existence, starting as they did without organization and without school buildings. The schools are organized into three departments: primary, intermediate and grammar. The course in the primary department is three years; in the intermediate two years, and in the grammar department it is three years. The tuition embraces a thorough course in the common branches, including physiology, algebra, botany, book-keeping, United States and English history. In November, 1884, written examinations of every pupil in school, from

*No report.

the second to eighth grades, were held. These with the photographs of the board of education, groups of the teachers and of the school buildings were sent to the World's Industrial and Cotton Centennial Exhibition at New Orleans, and placed in the educational department, for which the Jackson schools received an award. The first graduates from the Jackson City graded schools were in 1882, when there were nine; in 1883 there were six; in 1884, twelve; in 1885, eighteen white and three colored; in 1886, eighteen white and two colored pupils. The board of education, consisting of W. P. Robertson, J. H. Duke, James O'Connor, W. F. Alexander and E. S. Mallory, are men well suited for their places. Frank M. Smith, superintendent; F. P. Elliott, principal of Grammar Hall; Fannie Harper, principal of Primary Hall, and A. R. Merry (colored), with their assistants, are enjoying well earned reputations.

The public schools of Madison County were organized in 1873, under B. R. Campbell, as county superintendent. He was followed by Dr. J. D. Mason, in 1875–76; Alfred Oliver was superintendent from 1876 to 1878, and W. D. Meriwether from 1878 to 1880. W. G. Cockrill has been superintendent since that date. From a feeling of unfriendliness to positive opposition in some sections the schools have grown in much favor. The following tabular statement shows the increase under the various headings, as far as the reports are obtainable:

SCHOLASTIC POPULATION ENROLLMENT.

YEAR.	MALE.		FEMALE.		ATTEND-ANCE.	LENGTH IN DAYS.
	White.	Colored.	White.	Colored.		
1878	4,185	4,070	3,188	2,776	3,472	77
1879						
1880	5,435	5,308	2,240	1,140	3,268	90
1881	5,684	5,729	2,862	2,965	3,972	100
1882						
1883	4,818	5,267	4,054	3,715	not given	100
1884	5,141	5,728	2,882	2,994	4,172	102
1885	5,047	5,475	4,079	3,721	4,793	90
1886	5,500	5,383	3,070	3,080	4,390	120

YEAR.	NO. TEACHERS.	PAID IN SALARIES.	TOTAL RECEIPTS.	VALUE OF SCHOOL PROP.
1878	118	$13,338 35	$18,686 59	$4,050 00
1879				
1880	95	11,484 33	15,357 02	5,270 00
1881	68	12,117 07	16,184 69	8,221 00
1882				
1883	151	19,198 63	26,619 93	9,373 45
1884	97	12,692 62	24,971 70	10,568 22
1885	130	16,466 11	28,617 45	9,100 00
1886	115	16,072 18	23,705 91	7,026 77

Madison County has a school term of about six months in the year, and school-houses suitable for all.

The First Baptist Church of Jackson was organized according to the articles of faith of that church on January 29, 1837, by Rev. John Finlay and Rev. Peter S. Gayle. The following members signed the articles: H. M. Finlay, Mary Armour, Wm. Evans, Moses H. Prewitt, Mary B. Gannaway, Jenet Lake, Richard Rawlings, Nancy W. Evans, Wm. F. Still, G. York, Mrs. York and Mary J. York, all of whom are now dead. To Dr. Finlay is the church indebted for its organization in West Tennessee. Dr. Finlay was born March 10, 1794, in Scotland, and graduated at the University of Glasgow. In 1835 he came to West Tennessee and settled near Jackson. He superintended the Female Academy during the week and preached on Sundays at Cane Creek, Ararat, Denmark and at other points. Dr. Finlay was the first pastor, serving one year and three months, and was succeeded by Rev. Gayle, who served about eight months. Dr. Finlay again became pastor in October, 1838, and served as such till January, 1841. Rev. Gayle served as pastor in 1840, and again in 1844-45. In the early part of the year 1841, Rev. C. C. Conner became pastor and served the church for one year. There was a large increase in membership during his pastorate. Rev. Henry L. Pettus served the church in 1846, and Rev. G. D. Martin in 1847. Rev. A. J. Spivey became pastor in 1848 and served two years. During his pastorate, through the preaching of Rev. J. R. Graves, the church was greatly strengthened, so much so that the congregation was enabled to have preaching every Sabbath. Rev. George Tucker served the church from 1850 to 1852. At this time the church took very decided ground against the sale and use of ardent spirits. Rev. J. W. Miller became pastor in 1852, but severed his connection in a short time, when Rev. Abner Morrill, then tutor in West Tennessee College began preaching, and served the church till 1855. Rev. D. H. Selph, president of Madison College at Spring Creek, preached once a month till 1857, when Rev. Aaron Jones became pastor, and served two and a half years. It was during his pastorate an unfortunate dissension arose. Rev. J. R. Hamilton became pastor in 1860, and served about one year. Regular services were not held during the period of the war. Rev. A. J. Hall became pastor in October, 1865, and served till November 3, 1866. The church at this time was weak, but Rev. Hall did much to collect the scattered fragments of the once strong church. Rev. J. F. B. Mays served the church as pastor from June 4, 1867, to January 1, 1873. He found the church with about fifty members and left it with 196. Dr. C. R. Hendrickson became pastor August 15, 1873, and served till his death, October 21, 1881. It was in the beginning of his pastorate that the new church was begun. The building committee consisted of Dr. Hendrickson, Abner Lawler, M. Corbett and Dr. A. B. Powell. The financial committee consisted of D. W. Hughes, A. S. Sayle and Thomas E. Glass. The work was begun in 1874, but owing to financial depression the work was not completed till 1885. The church now has an excellent building worth from $8,000 to $10,000. Rev. E. B. McNeil served the church as pastor from February, 1882, to September of the same year. An unfortunate selection for pastor resulted in dissensions and a loss of about fifty members of the church. In October, Rev. McNeil was again recalled, and served acceptably till his successor, Rev. J. L. Vass, was chosen in March, 1885. The church now has regular preaching every Sabbath, also maintains a Sabbath-school, and is in a healthy condition spiritually and financially.

The first preaching at Ararat by a Baptist minister, was done by Rev. John Finlay, in 1837. The church was organized at this place in 1851, and a church erected in 1871. The trustees at that time being Sandy Cole, J. W. Shelton and C. Buntin. The church numbers ninety-eight members, and has property worth $500. Rev. M. A. Carthcart is pastor.

The church at Denmark numbers thirty-six members, with J. P. Kincaid as pastor. The church at that place was erected in 1871. The trustees of the church at that time were Jerry ———, W. Moddell and Joe Newbern. Rev. Finlay preached for the people of Denmark in 1837.

The church at Maple Spring was organized in 1849. The membership now is 122. The house of worship was erected in 1857. T. J. Fuller, Andrew Derrybery, Thomas Anderson, A. W. Fuller and Henry Jones, were the first trustees. The church has property worth $1,600. Rev. E. B. McNeil is pastor.

The church at Woodland numbers eighty-five members, with church property valued at $1,000. It is under the pastoral care of J. P. Kincaid.

The church at Cane Creek was organized in 1846. The first preaching at this point was by Rev. Finlay, in 1837–38. R. J. Jennings now serves as pastor. The present membership is thirty-eight. The ground on which the present church stands was deeded to the deacons of the church, in 1871, by H. W. Shelton. Central Jackson Church was organized in 1880, by Dr. Frederick Howard. This church is near the public square, and the membership reported in 1885, was 157. By the clerk's report, Clover Creek Church was constituted in 1826. The membership is 173, with J. P. Kincaid as pastor. The church at Independence numbers 113 members. It belongs to the Unity Baptist Association. The church at Liberty Grove numbers fifty-five members. The house was erected in 1854, Lewis Newsom, C. Nanny and Washington Shufeld being deacons at that time. Meridian Creek Church was constituted in 1881, and has a membership of thirty-eight. The church at Pinson was constituted in 1869. The membership is seventy-three. The Baptist Church at Pleasant Ridge numbers thirty-nine members. It belongs to the Unity Baptist Association. Friendship is a church of forty members. Its pastor is Rev. G. A. West. The church property is valued at $800. The church at Lavenia numbers ninety-four members. It owns church property worth $1,040. The church at New Liberty was constituted in 1884. Its membership is thirty-four. The church at Pleasant Plains numbers 122 members, with E. B. McNeil as pastor. The Church property is valued at $1,000. The church at Poplar Corner was organized in 1878. The membership is 145, and church property is valued at $1,000. The church at Spring Creek numbers 111 members. Their church property is valued at $800. There is also a church of nine members at Oak Grove.

The first Methodist Church in Jackson was organized at the court house in the fall of 1826, with eight members. Among them were Joseph Douglas and wife, Wyatt Epps and wife, and Robert Brown. The society was organized by Rev. Thomas Neeley. Services were either held at private houses or at the court house till the building of Temperance Hall about 1831. In 1851 this old church was sold by A. W. Jones, J. C. Sharp and Milton Brown, trustees of the church, to Jackson Sons of Temperance, for $1,900, and the lot where the present church stands was purchased. On this a new church was erected by the Brown brothers and Newells. Recent additions have been made to the church to the amount of $10,000. It is furnished with a pipe organ and seated with chairs, and is one of the most elegantly furnished in the city. The membership of the church is 352. It also maintains a flourishing Sunday-school. There are Methodist Churches in both East and West Jackson, the membership of the two aggregating about 250. The church property of the two is valued at $2,000.

The Jackson Circuit contains four churches, and has a membership of over 400. The church property of the circuit is valued at $5,000.

The Spring Creek Circuit has four churches, and a membership of nearly 400, and property worth over $5,000.

The Mifflin Circuit contains four churches, and has a membership of 328, and church property worth $2,100. Pinson Circuit has 600 members and eight churches, and church property valued at $7,000. This vigorous branch of the church has a membership in the county of nearly 2,500, and houses in almost every part of the county.

The presbytery of Western District held its first session at New Shiloh Church, near Humbolt, on November 6, 1829. The churches within the bounds of the presbytery were twelve in number. The delegate to that presbytery from Jackson was James Greer. The church at that time numbered thirty-three members. The first ministers to preach at Jackson were David Kerr and Thomas Lynch. In 1830 the presbytery took decided grounds on the question of intemperance, and resolved itself into a temperance society. At the same time it took a stand on the slavery question, not as a political question, but as a moral one. It was intended to look to the spiritual welfare of the slave. It was resolved that the churches take up an annual collection on the Fourth of July, or the Sabbath nearest to it, for the " Colonization Society. It was believed that a new native party Christianized could be transplanted into the bosom of their native land, the Dark Continent, and thus become a mighty factor in communicating the gospel to the benighted millions of Africa." This church also took an early stand for an educated ministry. In 1831 the presbytery was held in the court house in Jackson. The first Presbyterian Church built in Jackson was in the early part of 1830. This has since been replaced by an elegant house worth at least $10,000. The members of this church have already embraced the leading families of Jackson. The present pastor is Rev. J. H. Nall, D. D. The membership of the church is 312. A flourishing Sabbath-school is also maintained. The church at Denmark was formerly called Hopewell. This was organized about 1827 or 1828. In 1829 its membership numbered eighteen. The church at that place was built on a lot purchased from Joab Wilson by John Wharton, John Trigg, John Stetson, John Johnson, John Ingram, Benj. Tyson, and Evans Mabrey, in April, 1833. The membership is 127, with S. W. Newell, pastor. The Presbyterians have a church at Spring Creek also, but its strength is not reported.

St. Luke's Parish, Jackson, was organized July 23, 1832, at the Masonic Hall, Rev. Thomas Wright, recently from North Carolina, presiding, and the following persons signed the articles of association: Maj. Andrew L. Martin, Robert Hughes, Jacob Perkins, J. H. Rawlings, Dr. Lewis Pender, Dr. Erasmus D. Fenner, John M. Fenner, William Taylor, Col. Joseph H. Talbot, James Miller, Dr. Wm. E. Butler, Dr. Atlas Jones, Hon. Joshua Haskell, Wm. Stoddert, Micajah Antrey, Mrs. Sophia Perkins and Mrs. Eliza G. Vaulx. Five vestrymen were elected at this time. August 6, Rev. John Chilton was chosen rector, who served both St. Luke and Brownsville till 1834. After one year the Rev. Thomas West was called to the parish, and remained through 1836–37. From 1832 to 1836 preaching was held at the court house. After February, 1837, Rev. West preached twice a month at the male academy, occasionally at the residence of Dr. John G. Chalmers, Mount Pinson, and at Col. Samuel Dickens', near Spring Creek. Rev. West resigned his charge at the close of 1837. At the convention of the diocese, held at the court house in 1835, it was found that but two members lived in Jackson. An effort was made to build a church in 1836, but failed. The parish had no rector from 1837 to 1840. A few services were held by Rev. Abednego Stephens, in the fall of 1838, at the Methodist Church, and at the same place by Bishop Otey in 1839. In 1840 Rev. Chilton returned and preached once a month till his death, in August of that year. In 1842 Rev. Oliver H. Staples became rector, but resigned in about six months on account of ill-health. During his rectorship a Sunday-school was established, which is still maintained. Services were again held at the court house. From July, 1843, to January 1849, Rev. Louis Jansen was rector, serving the parishes both at Jackson and Brownsville. He resided for three years at Jackson, then at Brownsville. He also taught a female school. June 27, 1844, a lot was purchased of Granderson Spurlock, for $450, and the church edifice erected at a cost of $2,300. The brick work was done by John R. and Thomas G. Norvell, the wood work by W. F. Hampton and Francis Fogg, the painting by Jesse Russell and James A. Marks. It was ready for services, though not completed, in the fall of 1845. The convention of the diocese was held in this church in July, 1846. In April, 1849, Rev. John W. McCulloch, D. D., of Indiana, became rector, and held the position in connection with a professorship in West Tennessee College till his resignation in June, 1854. The church was completed by the building of pews and a chancel, and furnished with an organ and bell, and was consecrated by the bishop May 14, 1854. In October, 1851, the parish was favored with a visit by the Right Rev. Wm. M. Green, of Mississippi, who confirmed eleven persons. April 23, 1855, Rev. John A. Harrison, of Ashwood, Tenn., became rector. In that year a parsonage was erected on a five-acre lot given by James L. Talbot, at a cost of about $3,350. In the early history of this parish, the parishioners labored under many difficulties from want of means and members. In 1837 the only communicants were Samuel Dickens and wife Fanny, Mrs. Ann Fenner and three daughters—Mrs. Eliza G. Vaulx, Mrs. Matilda Coor Pendler and Mrs. Indiana McKnight. The success of the church is largely due to the devotion of its female members; foremost among them was Mrs. Eliza G. Vaulx, who abounded in every good work from 1832 to her death in 1845. Rev. Dr. Harrison resigned December 14, 1880, to accept a call to Trinity Church, Demopolis, Ala. A recess chancel was added to the church building in

1869 at a cost of $1,500. In July, 1874, the rectory and grounds in the suburbs were sold, and the rectory grounds adjoining the building were purchased in August following. Dr. F. A. Shoup became rector February 21, 1881, and remained till February following, when he resigned to accept a call at New Orleans. Dr. Geo. W. Durnbell took charge of the parish February 15, 1882, and continued in charge till September 23, 1883. During his rectorship the church was enlarged, remodeled and beautified at a cost of about $7,000. Dr. Durnbell resigned to accept St. James', Milwaukee, Wis., and Rev. George W. Hinkle took charge of the parish February 17, 1884. The convention of the diocese was held at St. Luke's Church in May, when 240 communicants and everything in hopeful and prosperous condition was reported.

On February 19, 1872, the organization of the first Cumberland Presbyterian Church of Jackson was effected. The articles of faith were signed by W. M. Dunaway, Sarah E. Dunaway and forty-three other members. The matter of organizing a church in Jackson was brought before the West Tennessee Synod, in 1868, by Rev. W. M. Dunaway. The proposition met the approval of the synod, and financial aid was promised. Revs. W. M. Dunaway and Pope, and B. G. McClesky were chosen a committee with power to begin the work. A lot was purchased on College Street, between Church and Royal, for $800. A building committee, of W. M. Dunaway, W. K. Walsh, John Y. Keith and J. W. Anderson, were appointed, who began at once to raise funds for a house of worship. A brick building, 36x65 feet, was begun and enclosed in 1871, when the work ceased temporarily for want of funds, but was resumed and the house completed in 1872. The dedicatory services were held in the church February 18, 1872. Rev. G. W. Mitchell preached the sermon. James W. Anderson, James F. Latham and Thomas B. Anderson were chosen elders. The deacons were Wm. D. Moxey, E. B. Carter and J. K. Landis. Rev. C. W. Mitchell was chosen first pastor. The number of communicants is now 160. There are good Cumberland Presbyterian Churches at Mount Tabor, Claybrook and Ebenezer.

The first church building by the Church of Christ was erected in Jackson, on the corner of Main and Cumberland Streets. This house is a neat frame building, about 40x50 feet, and it was completed in May, 1867. The erection of the house is due to J. D. Bond, B. F. Bond, R. W. Bond, R. W. Andrews, S. D. Andrews and G. B. Metcalf, who were the only male members then living in the city. The first sermon was preached by Elder T. W. Caskey, in May, 1867. No regular services were held till October, 1867. The first services were conducted without a pastor, by R. W. Bond. The first additions to the church were under the preaching of Elder R. B. Trimble. G. Hawkins and wife were the first members added. In May, 1868, R. F. Bond and R. W. Andrews were chosen elders, and J. D. Bond and J. W. Foster were chosen deacons. J. R. Wilkinson was appointed deacon in place of J. D. Bond, resigned, and W. B. McNabb was added to the number. The trustees chosen for the church were J. R. Wilkinson, Franklin Wilson and C. F. Landis. The membership of the church is about eighty in number.

The first worship by the Catholics in Jackson was in 1861. At that time there were but six families living in the place. Services were held first at the house of Mrs. Teague, near where Dr. Neely now lives. Father Daley was one of the first priests. A house and lot on the corner of Church Street, between Main and Lafayette, was soon after purchased for about $3,000, but unfortunately this was burned down. The lot was afterward sold, and the grounds on Royal Street, extending from Main to Baltimore, were purchased. The church has since built an elegant house of worship, priest's residence, and also has a parochial school. Four Sisters are employed in teaching. The membership of the church is now quite large, and they own property worth at least $25,000. The present priest is Father Abbot. The Catholics also own their own cemetery, which covers ten acres of ground.

MADISON COUNTY.

Frederick W. Adamson, clerk of the Madison County Court, was born in Jackson, Tenn., February 17, 1850, being the son of Greenbury and Elizabeth L. (Clark) Adamson, natives, respectively, of Maryland and Tennessee. His father, while yet single, came to Tennessee in 1830, locating at Charlotte, Dickson County, where he married, and in 1833 came to Jackson. He followed blacksmithing for a few years, and then engaged in the drug business, which he followed until the late war, and which considerably impoverished his property. He finally retired from business, and in 1876 died in Paris, Tenn. Frederick W. was reared and educated in this city, and early in life began clerking. He first entered the drug store, and later the mercantile business, and then, for twelve years or more, served as book-keeper for Smith & Stegall, wholesale grocers, and was also for two years book-keeper for J. T. McCutchen, cotton manufacturer. He has for a number of years been secretary of the Jackson Building & Savings Association. In August, 1886, he was elected, on the Democratic ticket, to his present official position. He is a member of the K. of P. and K. of H. fraternities, and is a vestryman of the Episcopal Church. March 12, 1874, he married Miss Susan E. Sneed, a native of Texas, who died in November, 1881, leaving two children: Benjamin G. and Elizabeth Helen.

William F. Alexander, shoe merchant, of Jackson, Tenn., and a native of that city, was born on the 3d of February, 1844, son of William and Elizabeth (Paramore) Alexander, who were born in South and North Carolina respectively. The father came to Jackson, Tenn., in the thirties, and was a successful carpenter. He was captain of the militia in Jackson in 1840, and was mayor of the town a number of terms before and after the late war. He died January 24, 1878. William F. has always made Jackson his home. When the war broke out he enlisted in Company H, Sixth Regiment Tennessee Infantry, Confederate States Army, and served as a private two years. In 1868 he engaged in the retail shoe business in Jackson, and has continued that occupation to the present time. He has the largest and best stock of goods in his line in the city, and is doing well financially. He is a Democrat, and has been a member of the city council for the past five years. He is a Mason— Knights Templar degree, and belongs to the K. of P., the K. of H., and A. O. U. W. Mary E. Hughes became his wife in November, 1868. She is a native of Hardeman County, Tenn., and is the mother of six children: John P., William F., J. R., Robert E., Elizabeth and Mary F.

Daniel R. Allison was born in Smith County, Tenn., January 15, 1821, and is the second member of a family of seven sons and six daughters, born to William and Mary (Ellison) Allison. Of this family but two are living, our subject, and one sister. The father was born in South Carolina, and immigrated with his parents to Tennessee when a small boy. He was reared in Smith County, and after his marriage settled at Middleton, Tenn. In 1833 or 1834 he moved to Madison County, where he followed farming. He died at his son Joseph's home December 21, 1878. His wife was born in Kentucky, and died in 1872. Daniel R. Allison has made farming his chief business through life. June 29, 1842, he married Nancy Watson, daughter of John Watson. Of thirteen children born to them but six are living: Mary J. (Mrs. Hogans), Beuna Vista A., Louisa (Mrs. Robertson), Virginia, Fannie Bell and James M. The mother of this family was born in Carroll County February 25, 1826. In April, 1864, Mr. Allison enlisted in Col. Newsom's regiment of Tennessee Cavalry, and was at Brice's Cross Roads. He accompanied Hood throughout his Tennessee raid, and was at the battles of Franklin and Nashville, and served with distinction until the close of the war. He is a Democrat, and owns 235 acres of land about eleven miles southeast of Jackson. He and Mrs. Allison are members of the Methodist Episcopal Church South.

Adolphus G. Andrews, M. D., was born in Henderson County, Tenn., in 1833, and is the son of Gray B. and Sallie (Harmon) Andrews. The father was born in North Carolina in 1797, and came to Tennessee with his parents when eight years old. He was a carpenter in his early life, his latter days being spent on the farm; he died in Henderson County in 1879. The mother of our subject was born in Montgomery County, Tenn., in 1810, and was the mother of thirteen children—two daughters and eleven sons. She died in 1865. The grandfather of our subject, Athelston Andrews, was born in North Carolina in 1761, and came to Tennessee in 1805; he was reared on the sea by a sea captain; at the age of fourteen he volunteered in the Revolutionary war; his wife was Polly (Jones) Hill, of North Carolina, and became the mother of eight children. Her first husband, Mr. Hill, was killed by a runaway negro. The grandparents died in 1839 and 1842, respectively. The maternal grandfather, John Harmon, was a native of North Carolina, born in 1770 and died in 1851. His wife was Elizabeth Baker, of South Carolina. Our subject was reared on a farm, remaining until 1861, when he enlisted in Company H, Twenty-seventh Tennessee Regiment (Confederate), and remained until the close of the war. He was wounded and was rendered unfit for duty for nine months. He joined N. B. Forrest's cavalry in 1862, and was with him at the close of the war. He read medicine before the war, and two years after the war was spent in reading medicine and farming. He attended the University of Louisville in 1868–69 and 1869–70, graduating in the latter year. He then located in Decatur County and practiced three years, then went to Henderson County and practiced until 1880, when he moved to Madison County, and in 1881 located at Spring Creek, and has done a large practice up to the present time. In 1865 he married Miss Mary E. Williams, daughter of Dr. D. H. and Susan Williams. She was born in Henderson County July 9, 1840, and is the mother of nine children—three daughters and six sons—two sons are dead. He and wife are members of the Missionary Baptist Church; he has been a member of the Masonic Order for twenty-nine years, and is strictly Democratic in politics.

John C. Askew was born in North Carolina March 18, 1839. His father was Augustus Askew, a native of the same State, born in 1808, and while yet there married Elizabeth Watford. In 1845 he moved to this county, locating near Norwood. He was a prosperous farmer, and died about 1868. The mother was a North Carolinian, and died in this county in 1864. Both father and mother were most estimable people. John C. was reared a farmer, and has since followed that calling. When the late war broke out he joined the Confederate Army, enlisting in the Sixth Tennessee Confederate Regiment. He fought at Shiloh, Chickamauga and Resaca, and was wounded at Chickamauga and thereby disabled for six months. At Resaca he was wounded and disabled two months. He served through and was surrendered at Greensboro, N. C. January 11, 1865, he married Miss Louisa C., daughter of V. B. Woolfolk, who has borne her husband four children, two now living: Julia R. and Floyd V. Mrs. Askew was born in this county in 1839. Mr. Askew is a Democrat, and he and lady belong to the Missionary Baptist Church. He owns 105 acres of land at Spring Creek, fourteen miles northeast of Jackson. He is one of the best citizens of the county.

Joseph D. Askew, of the firm of R. W. Swett & Co., merchants at Spring Creek, was born in North Carolina in 1842, and came to Tennessee with his father when two years old. The father, Alexander Askew, was born in North Carolina. The mother, Martha (Watford) Askew, was born in North Carolina, and is the mother of eleven children, and our subject is the only one living. The father died in 1873, his widow following him in 1876. Our subject was reared on a farm and remained until 1856, when he came to this village and began clerking, remaining until May, 1861, when he enlisted in the Confederate service, and remained until May, 1865. He was wounded while on the skirmish line near Mount Pleasant, Tenn., which rendered him unfit for duty seven weeks; he also received a slight wound caused by a falling limb during the battle of Shiloh. In July, 1865, he began merchandising in this village, the firm being Haughton & Askew, and continued until 1869, when he sold out and returned to his farm, and in 1873 he resumed business at this place, and with the exception of a few months continued up to the present time. In 1865 he married Mary J. Haughton, of this village, daughter of Geo. W. and Harriet (Barnett) Haughton. She was born in this place in 1844, and is the mother of four children—one daughter and three sons—of whom the three sons are deceased. He owns in this county about 1,100 acres of good land. The Askew family are of Scotch-Irish descent; in politics he is strictly Democratic.

Charles B. Baker, farmer and magistrate, was born in Jefferson County, Tenn., June 17, 1828. His grandfather, John Baker, was a native of North Carolina, and was an early immigrant to Tennessee. He died in East Tennessee, where he had located, the date of his death not being known. His son, John Baker, Jr., was born in East Tennessee, and was there married to Martha Mills, and they became the parents of three sons and two daughters, the subject of this sketch being the third member of the family. The father was a manufacturer of gunpowder, and followed that calling a number of years. He was also engaged in flat-boating from the upper Tennessee River to New Orleans during a certain season of the year, and also followed farming. He was a Confederate soldier, and at the close of the late war settled in West Tennessee. He died at the home of our subject, July 16, 1873. The mother died in Madison County in the winter of 1865. Charles B. Baker was reared on a farm, and has served his county and district as deputy sheriff, constable and magistrate for a period of fifteen years. He enlisted in the Confederate Army in the First Tennessee Regiment, under C. J. C. Carter, and was at Chickamauga, Resaca, Atlanta, and through the Georgia campaign. December 27, 1847, he was married to Nancy A., daughter of Thomas Elmore, a farmer. Mr. and Mrs. Baker became the parents of the following children: Joseph W., Michael T., Sallie A., Margaret E., Emma and Charles. Mrs. Baker was born in Jefferson County, Tenn., about 1831. Mr. Baker is a Democrat, and a member of the I. O. O. F. He owns 200 acres of land, and is one of the largest potato growers in West Tennessee.

H. Baum, Sr., a grocery merchant of Jackson, Tenn., is a native of Germany. He was born in 1853, and came to the United States in 1880; located in Jackson and began the confectionery business on a small scale. In 1883 he removed into the present large and commodious store room, where he now conducts a paying grocery business, carrying a large and select stock of staple and fancy groceries, queensware, etc.; also doing a wholesale business in tropical fruits. November 9, 1884, he married Josephine Loeb, of Ripley, Tenn. They have one son, Herbert J. Subject is a Mason, and a member of the K. of H. and K. of L. Himself and wife are Congregationalists in religious views.

Evander M. Betts, a prominent merchant of Claybrook, was born in Davidson County, Tenn., in 1833, and is the son of John J. and Ruth (Glasgow) Betts. The parents are also natives of this State. The Betts family are among the first settlers of Davidson County. The father was a farmer in the latter part of his life, his early days being spent in milling. Ten children blessed their union—three daughters and seven sons—of whom two daughters and two sons are living. The father moved to Mississippi in 1845, and there remained until his death, which occurred in 1849. He was in the war of 1812, and furnished one son for the Florida Indian war and two for the Mexican war. His widow followed him in death in 1883. Our subject was reared to manhood on the farm, leaving it at the age of twenty-one, and engaged in different pursuits until 1861, when he volunteered in the quartermaster's department, and remained until 1862, when he enlisted in the Fifty-first Tennessee Regiment and there remained until 1864, when he was wounded at Atlanta, Ga., which rendered him unfit for soldier duty the remainder of the war; yet he rendered the Southern Confederacy all possible aid otherwise until the close. Since the war he has been engaged in farming, milling and stock-trading, until 1875, when he began merchandising in the village, and continues up to the present time. In 1861 he married Miss Catherine T. Bushy. She was born in this State about 1841, and is the mother of one child, that died at the age of nineteen. The mother died in 1865. In 1866 he married Lou Boswell, of this State, and daughter of Edward Boswell. She was born in 1833, and is the mother of one child, named Emily A. Himself and wife are members of the Cumberland Presbyterian Church. November 25, 1886, his daughter, Emily A., was united in marriage to Wm. R. Britt. Our subject is a member of the Masonic order, and also of the K. of G. R. In politics he is Democratic.

George B. Black, a prominent farmer, was born in Madison County, Tenn., on the 13th of September, 1844. His father, Cyrus Black, was born in South Carolina September 18, 1800, and emigrated to Tennessee in early life. He married Emily Baily, who was born in Virginia. Their family consisted of one daughter and our subject. Cyrus Black made farming his chief business in life, and died in Madison County October 5, 1863. His wife died in 1857. George B. Black received common school advantages, and has followed agricultural pursuits as his chief occupation. He enlisted in the Confederate Army in the Fourteenth Tennessee Cavalry under Col. Richardson. He was with Forrest's command, and did service in Mississippi, Tennessee, Alabama and Georgia, and was with the advance guard in front of Hood during his Tennessee campaign. He was at Franklin, and was wounded at Nashville, which disabled him for further duty during the remainder of the war. He was married in Madison County, December 24, 1868, to Miss Emma Harrison, daughter of James Harrison, a mill-wright by trade. They have four children: Lizzie B., Anna A., Grace V. and Ada. Mr. Black is a Democrat, and he and Mrs. Black are members of the Cumberland Presbyterian Church. He owns 450 acres of land, 350 acres of which is in the home farm.

James W. Blackmon is a native of this county, and was born September 30, 1850. His father, William Blackmon, was born in North Carolina, and was brought by his parents to Tennessee, when twelve years of age. The family located in Madison County, and here William was reared. Upon reaching manhood he married Martha H., daughter of Thomas Rollins, who bore him twelve children, of whom only four are now living—James W. and three sisters. James W. was the fifth of the family. The father was a farmer and died June 7, 1882. The mother was a North Carolinian and at the age of nine years was brought to Madison County. James W., like his father, is a farmer. He was liberally educated in English, and attended a commercial course at Evansville, Ind. He chose farming as his occupation and has continued thus to the present. In 1885 he opened his general store at Spring Creek. May 13, 1875, he married Miss Nannie E., daughter of J. D. Pearson. She has given her husband this family: Sidney A., Ethel M. and J. D. (deceased). Mrs. Blackmon was born in Henderson County, Tenn., May 19, 1853. Her father was brought to that county when a small boy. James W. is a Democrat, a Mason (Master of Spring Creek Lodge, No. 193,) and he and lady are members of the Methodist Episcopal Church South. He owns a good farm of 280 acres, eleven miles northwest of Jackson.

F. E. Bond, a member of the firm of F. E. Bond & Co., the popular dry goods house of Jackson, is a native of this State, and was born in 1857. He is the son of F. A. and Eliza (Young) Bond, natives of North Carolina and Tennessee respectively. The father came to Tennessee when about five years of age, and was prosperous in early life, but afterward met with reverses that caused financial embarrassment. He died in September, 1886, leaving a widow and six children. Our subject spent his early life on the farm and received his education in the common schools. At the age of seventeen he came to this city, and engaged as clerk with F. H. Mayo & Co., remaining with them seven years, when Mr. Bond, in partnership with H. L. Penn, opened the business in which he has continued up to the present time. In 1881 Mr. Bond was united in marriage to Miss Etta Crawford, of this city, and daughter of Mark and Isabella Crawford. She was born in 1861, and is the mother of one child named Mark, who died in September, 1881. Mr. Bond is a true Democrat.

Sion W. Boon was born March 4, 1830; son of Benjamin and Annie (Winston) Boon, who were native North Carolinians. The father was born November 25, 1783, and was a farmer by occupation. He came to Tennessee about 1825 and located near Cotton Grove, where he died November 26, 1865. The mother died about 1831. Mr. Boon's second wife, Nancy Smith, died about 1853. Sion W. Boon was reared on his father's farm in Madison County, Tenn., and educated in the country schools. He began clerking at the age of twenty and continued the same until 1856, when he was elected circuit court clerk, and filled the office for eighteen years, thus illustrating his ability as an official and the esteem in which he was held by the people. Since retiring from official life he has been engaged in different pursuits, and in 1885 opened a family grocery in Jackson. He was married in 1856 to Louisa Pyles, a daughter of James M. and Nancy Pyles. She was born in 1836, and is the mother of nine children—two daughters and seven sons. Four of the children are yet living. Mrs. Boon died July 3, 1879, and in 1884 Mr. Boon married Amanda E. Smith, who was born about 1846, and is a daughter of James Smith. Mr. Boon votes the Democratic ticket.

John T. Botts, of the firm of Robertson & Botts, was born in Montgomery County, Ky., August 8, 1843, and is the son of Seth and Emily (Campbell) Botts, natives of Virginia and Kentucky. John T. was reared in his native State, and at the age of fourteen years began clerking in the mercantile business, continuing until after he had attained his majority. In April, 1866, he came to Jackson and entered into partnership with Mr. Robertson, and has continued thus until the present. December 1, 1868, he married Miss Lyde Tomlin, daughter of Hon. J. L. H. Tomlin, who has borne him three sons—two of whom are dead—and two daughters. Mr. Botts is a Democrat, a member of the Encampment of Odd Fellows, is Noble Grand of the subordinate lodge at Jackson, is a member of the K. of P., the K. of H., the A. O. U. W., and is a Knight Templar of the Masonic order, and one of the leading and substantial business men of Jackson.

Louis J. Brooks, editor and proprietor of the semi-weekly West Tennessee *Whig*, at Jackson, Tenn., was born August 24, 1853, at Lexington, Henderson Co., Tenn. He is one of four surviving members of a family of seven children born to the marriage of Rev. John Brooks and Sarah S. Acton. John Brooks was born in the Emerald Isle, in 1810, and when about thirteen years of age came to the United States and resided in Philadelphia two years. About this time he came to Tennessee, and resided in Nashville, and then Purdy, McNairy County, a few years, and finally located in Lexington, Henderson County. In 1867 he took up his abode in Jackson. He was married to a Miss Wilson, of McNairy County, and three children blessed their union, W. J., a merchant at Altus, Ark., being the only one living at the present time. Mrs. Brooks died and Mr. Brooks married our subject's mother. She is a native of Fincastle, Va., and is now residing in Jackson. The father was a local minister of the Methodist Church, and was a merchant of Jackson for many years. He was a prominent Mason and at one time, prior to the war, was director of the Tennessee State Bank. His death occurred at Jackson, in 1880. His son, Louis J. Brooks, graduated from the West

Tennessee College of Jackson, in 1872, with the degree of A. M. He then accepted the position of corresponding editor and general traveling agent for the *Plain Dealer*, published at Jackson, and after holding the position a few months, established the Lexington *Reporter*, which he very successfully edited about one year. He returned to Jackson, and in connection with Col. John T. Hogan, established the *Tri-Weekly Herald*, which after six months was merged into a daily and edited nearly two years; then owing to the failure of Mr. Brook's health he severed his connection with journalism and traveled about six months. After his return, he read law with Howell E. Jackson, a few months, and then (in 1875) became general manager of the *Whig and Tribune*, and continued the same about three years. The paper was then consolidated with the *Jackson Sun*, and he held a position on that paper for a few months, then purchased a half interest in the *Milan Exchange*, and with W. A. Wade published the paper about two years. He returned to Jackson about this time and bought a one-third interest in the West Tennessee *Whig*, but soon after (in July, 1883,) became sole proprietor and editor of the same. By January, 1885, the business had so increased that the semi-weekly was established. The *Whig* was first edited by Col. W. W. Gates, in 1844. In June, 1881, Mr. Brooks married Laura Blemken, of Evansville, Ind., but a native of Louisville, Ky. They are the parents of the following children: Ernest, Louise (deceased), Louis J., Jr. Mr. Brooks is a K. of P. and is one of Jackson's Second National Bank directors. He is ex-vice-president and has been one of the Tennessee Press Association. He also received appointment from Gov. Bates to the Mississippi River Convention held at Washington, D. C. He owns valuable city property and a tract of 120 acres of land in the county.

Finis E. Bryan, merchant, is a native of this county, and was born in 1842. His father, John T. Bryan, was born in Maryland, and came to West Tennessee in 1821, having lived the previous few years in Middle Tennessee. His occupation was farming, but he kept a land office in Jackson for some time, and was surveyor for many years. The mother, whose maiden name was Elizabeth Raines, was born in this State, and became the mother of ten children, nine of whom lived to be grown, and eight of whom are yet living. The father died in 1878, and the mother preceded him twelve years. Finis E. was reared to manhood on a farm, and in 1868 engaged in the mercantile business in this village, and has continued thus to the present time. He carries groceries and drugs, and has a profitable trade. In 1862 he entered the Confederate service in the company of Capt. (now Dr.) Murchison, of the Fifty-second Regiment, and served faithfully until the close of the war. He was twice taken prisoner, and was wounded in the left leg, which disabled him for a few weeks. In 1868 he married Miss F. E. Jett, who died in 1882, and the following year he married Miss Jennie Ducker, of this county. He is a Democrat, and a Methodist, and his wife is a Presbyterian.

Col. John W. Buford, clerk of the supreme court of Tennessee, at Jackson, was born in Williamson County August 24, 1836, and is the son of Spencer and Mary W. (Anthony) Buford, natives, respectively, of Virginia and Tennessee. His grandfather, James Buford, came to the State early in the present century, settling in Williamson County, where the father of Col. Buford was reared, educated and married, and his family were born. They were planters by occupation, and were useful and exemplary citizens. Col. Buford was reared in Williamson County, securing an academical education, and at the age of about nineteen years began the study of law under Judge David Campbell, and in due time graduated from the Lebanon (Tenn.) Law School, and was admitted to practice there in 1859. He removed to West Tennessee, and followed agricultural pursuits in Obion County until the breaking out of the late war, when, in 1861. he enlisted in Company H, Ninth Tennessee Confederate Infantry, and was elected captain of his company, which was known by the significant name of the Obion Avalanche. After twelve months' service as captain he was promoted to the position of lieutenant-colonel of his regiment, continuing there until the battle of Perryville, where he was dangerously wounded and captured by the Federals, and confined in military prisons until the middle of the year 1863, when he was exchanged. He rejoined his command at Shelbyville, Tenn., and officiated as lieutenant-colonel until the termination of the war. He then located in Williamson County, and there practiced his profession until 1872, when he came to Jackson, and has here since continued the practice. He has served as mayor of Jackson two terms, and in April, 1884, was appointed to his present position, a merited recognition of his standing in the community. In 1865 his marriage with Miss Emma S. Byers, of Kentucky, a niece of Gen. A. S. Johnston, was solemnized, and of this union there are three children, one son and two daughters. The Colonel is a Democrat, a member of the Masonic (Royal Arch Degree) and K. of P. fraternities, and himself and family are members of the Episcopal Church.

Ernest L. Bullock, attorney at law, of Jackson, Tenn., was born in Madison County, June 16, 1849; son of Micajah and Susan M. (Brown) Bullock, natives, respectively, of North Carolina and Tennessee. Micajah Bullock came to Tennessee in 1825, and located in Lexington, Tenn., where he soon after began practicing law. In 1835 he removed to Jackson, where he practiced law until his death, in August, 1872. He was more than ordinarily successful in the legal profession, and stood the peer of any lawyer in West Tennessee, or even in the State. He was extensively known and universally respected for his brilliant attainments and many good qualities. He was an old line Whig, in *ante bellum* days, and represented both Henderson and Madison Counties in the State Legislature, being a member of the committee that codified the laws of Tennessee, in 1858. Only two of his six children are now living: Anna R. (Mrs. R. A. Sneed), and Ernest L., who was reared in the county and secured a fair education. He took a partial course in the West Tennessee University, and at the age of seventeen accepted the position as deputy clerk of the supreme court at Brownsville, which position he held four years. He then entered the Lebanon Law School, and graduated in 1871. Since that time he has practiced in Jackson, and has met with good success. He is a Democrat, and in 1878 was nominated by his party, without opposition, for the office of attorney-general of Madison County. He was elected and served eight years, his district comprising Madison and Chester Counties. He is a K. of P., Past Commander of the local lodge, and is present Grand Inner Guard of the Grand Lodge of Tennessee. He is a member of the executive committee from Madison County, for the Eighth Congressional District, and is chairman of the county Democratic executive committee.

John D. Bumpus is a native of Williamson County, Tenn., born on the 6th of November, 1838. His father, A. A. Bumpus, was born in Person County, N. C., May 8, 1811, and immigrated to Tennessee in 1820. He located in Williamson County and was married at Springhill, Tenn., to Mary J. Potter. Of four sons born to them our subject is the eldest. The mother was born in Maury County, in 1816, and died in 1847. The father took for his second wife Miss E. T. Frazier, and four children blessed their union. A. A. Bumpus was a farmer, and in 1847 located in Madison County, where he now lives. John D. Bumpus, like his father, has been a tiller of the soil through life. He served in the Confederate Army in the Sixth Tennessee Infantry, Manny's brigade, Cheatham's division and Polk's command. He was captured at Point Rock, Ala., and was under parole for the period of two months. He was then exchanged and again entered the service, joining the Nineteenth Tennessee Cavalry under Col. J. M. Newson. He was in the battles of Guntown, Harrisburg, Murfreesboro, Perryville (Ky.), Pulaski (Tenn.), and many others. He served throughout the entire war and surrendered at Gainesville, Ala., May 18, 1865. February 13, 1861, he married Maggie E. Giles, daughter of Calvin Giles, a blacksmith and native of Middle Tennessee.   To Mr. and Mrs. Bumpus were born the following children: Mary Alice (Mrs. Smith), William L., Alexander A., Walter, Austin P., Johnnie D., Eddie, Robert, Mattie A., Georgie, Louise and Dovie. The mother was born in Cotton Grove, Tenn., June 28, 1838, and she and Mr. Bumpus are members of the Methodist Episcopal Church South. He is a Democrat, and owns 156 acres of land about nine miles from Jackson.

John W. N. Burkett is a native of Woodruff County, Ark., born January 26, 1854, son of Madison and Emily (Welch) Burkett, who were born in Tennessee.   John W. N. made his home in Arkansas until nineteen years of age; then came to Jackson, Tenn., where he completed his education, graduating with first honors in 1878.   The following October he engaged in the grocery business with G. H. Ramsey, continuing until January, 1883, when he engaged in his present business and has met with good success.   November 19, 1879, he married Miss Callie W. Robbins, of Haywood County, Tenn.   Mr. Burkett is a Democrat in his political views, and is alderman of the Fourth Ward, chairman of the finance committee and treasurer of the city of Jackson.   He is a Mason, Knights Templar degree, and he and wife are members of the Methodist Episcopal Church South.

William A. Caldwell, cashier of the First National Bank of Jackson, Tenn., was born in Greensboro, N. C., October 1, 1817, son of Thomas and Elizabeth (Doak) Caldwell, both natives of North Carolina, where they lived and died.   Subject was reared and educated in his native place. In 1833 he began clerical work as clerk in superior court clerk's office under his father, and in 1837 he engaged in the mercantile business with his brothers, which he followed successfully until 1853, when he was made cashier of a bank in his native place, in which business he engaged with good success until the war.   After the war he was upon finance committee of the North Carolina Railroad for about four years, and was treasurer of the road twenty months.   In the meantime he wound up his first banking business, which had been crippled by the misfortunes of war, and in 1872 came to Jackson and set upon foot the project for a savings bank. and the following year removed here with his family and opened up the Jackson Savings Bank, of which he was cashier.   August, 1874, the bank was merged into a national bank under present name, and Mr. Caldwell has been its efficient and faithful cashier ever since.   In 1849 he married Rachell Donnell, of North Carolina.   They have five children— two sons and three daughters.   Mr. Caldwell was originally an old line Whig in politics, but since the war has been a conservative Democrat, representing his district one year in the State Legislature in North Carolina. Himself and family are members of the Presbyterian Church. Mr. Caldwell is justly recognized as one among the most substantial and enterprising of Jackson's citizens, and to his long experience and fine business tact is due the eminent success of the banking institution with which he is so prominently identified.

Gen. Alexander W. Campbell, attorney at law, is the son of John W. and Jane E. (Porter) Campbell, and was born in Nashville June 4, 1828. His father was a native of Kentucky, and his mother of Tennessee, and in 1833 came to Jackson, Tenn., where Alexander W. was reared and educated. In the winter of 1847–48 he began the study of law under Judge A. W. O. Totten, and later attended the law school at Lebanon, from which institution he graduated in 1851, and the following year opened a law office in Jackson, and continued the practice until the war, when he was appointed, by Gov. Harris, assistant inspector-general of the provisional army of Tennessee, and as such mustered into the service the greater portion of the West Tennessee troops. Upon the transfer of the provisional army to the service of the Confederate Government, Gen. Campbell became colonel of the Twenty-third Regiment, under Gen. B. F. Cheatham, and in 1865 was promoted to a brigadier-general and placed in the command of Gen. Forrest in charge of the brigade which bore his name, retaining said command until the surrender. After the war Gen. Campbell resumed the practice of law in Jackson, and has thus been occupied until the present, having met with more than ordinary success. For the past quarter of a century he has been one of the foremost Democrats and leading practitioners of this portion of the State. January 12, 1852, his marriage with Miss Anne D., daughter of the distinguished lawyer, Dixon Allen, of Nashville, was solemnized, and to this union six children have been born, four of whom are now living: Mrs. Anne A. McIntosh, of Memphis; John W.; Katie F. and Alexander W. Gen. Campbell is a Knight Templar in Masonry, a member of the K. of P. and A. O. U. W. fraternities, and himself and wife are Episcopalians in religious belief.

James G. Carter, grocery and dry goods merchant of Jackson, Tenn., was born in North Carolina in 1854, and came to Tennessee about 1873. His parents, Joseph and Mary Carter, were born in North Carolina and Virginia, respectively. The father came to Tennessee about 1875, and was a carpenter by trade. James G. Carter was reared to manhood on a farm, and for a number of years (until 1876) followed different occupations. At the latter date he opened his grocery and dry goods store. He purchased his entire stock on credit, having only 50 cents in cash at the time he began business, and 43 cents of that was spent for tobacco license. He has succeeded well financially, and has a fine stock of goods and some city property also. In 1878 he married Maggie L. Ruffin, of Jackson. She was born in 1859, and is a daughter of Robert J. and Melissa A. Ruffin. Mr. and Mrs. Carter are the parents of two children— Floyd S. and Nellie B.—and are members of the Methodist Church. Mr. Carter is a member of the I. O. O. F., and is a Democrat in politics.

Stoddert Caruthers, attorney at law, of Jackson, Tenn., a native of Madison County, was born February 21, 1845, son of James and Frances E. (McCorry) Caruthers, natives, respectively, of Rockbridge County, Va., and East Tennessee. The father came to West Tennessee as a representative of several large land companies about 1819, and was engaged in his professional capacity as surveyor some years, locating in Jackson in 1821. He bought out the land owned by the companies he represented, and traded and dealt extensively in lands in West Tennessee and Mississippi until his death, in 1863. Our subject was reared to manhood in this his native county, securing a literary education at West Tennessee College. At a later period he graduated in law at Lebanon, Tenn. (in 1867), and commenced practice here the same year with Judge McCorry, continuing thus until the latter went on the bench, and has been connected with Mr. E. S. Mallory in the practice of his profession since 1871, and it may be justly said that Mr. Caruthers has contributed largely to the success and standing of this well-known law firm. Mr. Caruthers is and always has been a Democrat in politics. He served as a private in the late war in Company G, Ninth Tennessee Cavalry, two years. Mr. Caruthers is a member of the K. of P. and I. O. O. F. fraternities, and is recognized as one of the enterprising and successful citizens of Jackson, and a legal practitioner of high experience and ability.

Robert H. Cartmell was born in Jackson, Tenn., July 27, 1828. His father, Martin Cartmell, was born in Virginia November 2, 1797, and came to Tennessee with his mother. At the age of eighteen he enlisted in Gen. Jackson's body guard, and served in the Georgia and Florida campaign against the Indians. He was married to Margaret Neill, of Wilson County, who died October 24, 1820, having borne two daughters, who are both dead. In 1827 the father married Miss J. A. Sharp, and the fruits of their union were three sons and two daughters, our subject being the eldest member of the family. The father was a saddler by trade and owned several large farms, one of which was the finest in the county. Besides this, he owned a large number of slaves. He died at his home in Jackson July 4, 1864. The mother was born in Rutherford County in 1809, and is now living in Jackson. Robert H. Cartmell was raised in that town and graduated from the West Tennessee

College. He served a short time in the Confederate Army, but was discharged, at Tupelo, Miss., on account of disability. March 27, 1850, he married Miss M. J. Baldwin, daughter of Alfred Baldwin, and their union resulted in the birth of eight children, four of whom are living: Lizzie, Gaston B., Robert H. and Harry Martin. Mrs. Cartmell was born in Richmond County, N. C., and died at her present home May 31, 1865. Our subject is an old line Jacksonian Democrat and a member of the K. of P. and old school Presbyterian Church. He owns 800 acres of land one mile from Jackson.

Col. Robert I-o-h-nstone Chester was born in Carlisle, Penn., July 31, 1793. He was reared at Jonesboro, East Tenn., and was educated at the "old field" schools. He served in the war of 1812 as quartermaster of the Third Tennessee Regiment, being mustered in at Knoxville October 14, 1814. In 1816 he began merchandising, and in 1819 engaged in the tobacco business, in which he lost a fortune. In 1822 he was surveyor of Smith County. From 1824 to 1830 he was a merchant of Jackson, and from 1825 to 1833 was postmaster of the town. In 1835 he went to Texas, where he was appointed a colonel by Gov. Houston in the Texan revolution, but the victory of San Jacinto prevented further proceeding. He returned to Jackson in 1836, and was reappointed postmaster and appointed registrar of the western land district, and has been engaged in the land business much of the time since. In 1837 he was appointed by President Van Buren United States marshal for the western district, and served with one or more intermissions until 1861— sixteen years. He lost heavily during the war, in slaves and other property. He was elected to the Legislature in 1870 and re-elected in 1872, and has been a life-long Democrat, having been an intimate friend of Gen. Jackson, and having married the latter's niece, youngest daughter of Robert Hayes. In 1884 he was one of the Tennessee electors. He has been a member of the Masonic lodge since 1817, and is a Knight Templar. His first wife was Miss Elizabeth Hayes, by whom he had seven children: Mary Jane, John, Robert Hayes, Martha Butler, William Butler, Andrew Jackson and Samuel Hayes. His wife having died, Col. Chester married Mrs. Jane P. Donelson in 1855. During the late war his four sons served in the Confederate Army with conspicuous gallantry. Col. Chester has led a remarkable life, full of honor, usefulness, enterprise, benevolence and manhood, and has the fullest confidence and respect of all who know him. The great State has no better citizen.

Jay G. Cisco, editor and proprietor of the *Forked Deer Blade*, was born in the city of New Orleans, April 25, 1844, and is the son of Louis

J. and Loretta (Wezinski) Cisco, natives, respectively, of France and Austria. Jay G. was reared in his native city, and was prepared to enter college, when the war broke out. He enlisted in the Confederate Army, serving as a private, and in the secret service until the cessation of hostilities. He then secured an engagement as a newspaper correspondent, in the Northwest Territories, with Hancock and Custer; but in 1867 went to Europe, to visit his mother, Countess Ullenhoff, who is a resident of Austria, and upon his return to the United States, he engaged in the book business at Tuscaloosa, Ala., and came to Jackson in 1875, continuing the same business. In November, 1883, he established his present newspaper venture, which has proved highly successful and satisfactory. Independent Democracy is the politics of the paper. In January, 1879, Mr. Cisco was united in marriage with Miss Georgie Pursley, of Wilson County, Tenn. By a former marriage Mr. Cisco has a daughter, who is the wife of an aid-de-camp of Gen. Tosi, of the Austrian Army. Mr. Cisco is a member of the American Association for the Advancement of Science, and owns a valuable collection of prehistoric relics, and an excellent library of early American history.

Thomas Clark was born in Nashville, Tenn., in 1821. His father, James P. Clark, was born in Roane County, Tenn., and was a lawyer by profession. He was clerk of the supreme court of the State, at the time of his death, which occurred in 1863. His wife, whose maiden name was Susan McCorry, was born at Knoxville, Tenn., and became the mother of thirteen children, eleven of whom lived to be grown, and nine are living at the present time. The mother died in 1884. Thomas Clark resided in the city of Nashville until fifteen years of age. He then came to Jackson, and the first four years of his stay in this city were spent in clerking and reading law. At the early age of twenty, he obtained his license to practice, and in 1846 was appointed clerk of the chancery court, and held the office for twenty-five years. Since that time, he has been engaged in farming, and serving the people as justice of the peace. In 1861 he enlisted in the Confederate service, and served as quartermaster throughout the war. In 1845 he was married to Frances Patterson, of Jackson, daughter of Allen L. and Drucilla Patterson. She was born in Springfield, Tenn., in 1823, and became the mother of five sons and five daughters. Three sons and four daughters are yet living. Mr. and Mrs. Clark are members of the Episcopal Church, and he belongs to the I. O. O. F., and is a Democrat.

Maj. Edwin A. Clark, a prominent official of Jackson, was born in Charlotte, N. C., in 1826. His father, Jonas Clark, was born in Maryland, in 1759, and went to North Carolina, at an early age. He volunteered in the Revolutionary war, when eighteen years of age, and served four years. He afterward drew a pension of $220 per year, for his services. He came to Tennessee in 1830. His wife, whose maiden name was Ann Alexander, was born in North Carolina, in 1787, and was Jonas Clark's third wife. She and her husband were members of the Presbyterian Church, and belonged to the Steel Creek congregation. The father died in 1845, and his wife in 1858. Edwin A. Clark was reared on a farm, and at the age of fifteen left home and began clerking for $60 per annum. With the exception of ten months, spent in the Mexican war, he clerked until 1849, but with increased wages, after the first year. Some time after the close of the Mexican war, he went to California, where he remained until 1851. In 1852 he married Martha Childress, of Springfield, Tenn., daughter of George and Martha (Murdock) Childress. Mrs. Clark was born in 1835, and is the mother of three children—one daughter and two sons. Mrs. Clark died in 1869, and in May, 1881, Maj. Clark married Mary M. Black, of Henderson County, daughter of Thomas N. and Mary Black. She was born in 1843. Mr. Clark and his brother engaged in the mercantile business at Cotton Grove, about 1852, and continued the same for six years. He then spent four years doing business at different points. In 1862 he, as captain, and S. D. Barnett, as first lieutenant, assisted in the organization of the Fifty-first Tennessee Regiment, and Mr. Clark was chosen major. He was captured at Fort Donelson, and was exchanged after the seven days' fight in and around Richmond. On account of physical disability, he was unable to engage longer in the service, and returned home and resumed mercantile business at Spring Creek, in partnership with Herron & Mason, continuing five years. The following two years were spent in farming, and he then came to Jackson and began speculating in cotton, which resulted in financial embarassment. He then clerked for sometime, and held the office of tax collector during 1874–75, and in 1876 he was defeated by a Republican, for the sheriff's office, and in 1878 was elected county court clerk, and held the office eight years. He is at present a candidate for the office of comptroller of the State. He is a Democrat, and he and Mrs. Clark are members of the Presbyterian Church.

Stephen R. Conger, lumber dealer of Jackson, Tenn., and native of Madison County, was born October 13, 1853, son of Philander D. W. and Eliza J. (Chambers) Conger, natives respectively of Virginia and North Carolina. Stephen R. was reared to manhood in Jackson, and secured a good practical education. In May, 1873, he engaged in the lumber business in that place. His business was quite small at first, but has gradually increased until he is now the largest lumber dealer in the city or county. He employs twelve or thirteen hands, and has three large yards and a planing-mill. His annual business amounts to about $40,000. October 13, 1874, he married Amelia Cox, of Elkton, Ky. They have five children: Charles P., Lee W., Richard, Cora May and Frederick H. Mr. Conger is an unswerving Democrat in politics, and was alderman of Jackson one term. He belongs to the K. of H., K. of P. and I. O. O. F. fraternities, and he and wife are members of the Baptist Church.

Henry H. Cooper, of the firm of H. H. Cooper & Co., druggists of Jackson, Tenn., is a native of Louisiana, and is thirty-three years old. He came to Jackson in 1881, and was married in 1882. He engaged in the confectionery business in October, 1883, in which he has been very successful. In October, 1882, he became a member of the above named firm, and is doing a prosperous business. He is a Democrat, a member of the K. of H., and he and wife are members of the Episcopal Church.

William H. Croom, a prominent citizen and farmer of Madison County, was born Qctober 11, 1822, in Wayne County, N. C., and is one of eight sons and three daughters born to Charles and Siveal (Hines) Croom, our subject, six brothers and one sister, being the surviving members. The parents were married in their native place, Wayne County, N. C., and farmed there till they came to Madison County, Tenn., about 1827, and continued agricultural pursuits in this county until their deaths in 1863 and 1885, respectively. In 1839 our subject was married, and began farming on a tract of land in this county, given him by his father, but in 1861 located on his present home place of 655 acres, one mile south of Pinson, which he has well improved, and is in an excellent state of cultivation. At the commencement of the war he enlisted in the Thirteenth Tennessee Confederate Infantry, and served until 1864, when he was discharged, and has since devoted his attention to the cultivation and improvement of his farm. Our subject married, for his first wife, Caroline Carrington, native of this county, to whom four sons and two daughters were born. One of the sons died in the hospital at Atlanta, Ga., during the war (1863), and another is also deceased, while of the two living, one resides in Madison County, and the other in Arkansas. The daughters are both living. The mother of these children died about 1858, and he afterward married Virginia A. Anderson, a native also of this county, and to whom four sons and two daughters have been born, all still living, three of the sons residing in Arkansas, and the other in Mississippi, while the daughters are both at home. Mr. Croom is identified with the Democratic party. Mrs. Croom and family are members of the Methodist Church.

Dr. Richard R. Dashiell, postmaster of Jackson, Tenn., was born in Baltimore, Md., August 18, 1816. He is a son of Alfred H. and Ann (Ridgely) Dashiell, both natives of Maryland. The father emigrated West in 1837, locating first in Nashville, where he accepted the presidency of the Nashville Female College, being also a minister in the Presbyterian Church, and later officiated in his clerical capacity at Franklin and Shelbyville, and still later was president of the Rogersville College, of East Tennessee, until 1858, when he returned East and died in Brooklyn, N. Y., about 1882. Our subject was reared to manhood in his native city, securing a collegiate education at Amherst College, Mass. Early in life he began the study of medicine, with a view to making it a profession, and accordingly entered the medical department of the University of Pennsylvania, graduating in 1837. He commenced practice in the same year in Nashville, and continued until 1839, when he took charge of several large iron works in and below Clarksville, which he managed successfully eight years. In 1846 the Doctor removed to Jackson and entered regularly in the practice of his profession, in which he continued until the war, when he went out in 1861 as surgeon of the Sixth Regiment, Tennessee Confederate Infantry, serving in his professional capacity until 1863, when he resigned on account of failing health. After the war he resumed his practice here, in which he met with good and well deserved success until December, 1885, when he received the appointment to the postmastership at Jackson, and is now discharging the duties of this important position in a highly efficient and faithful manner. In 1841 the Doctor married Miss Louisa J. Kizer, of Stewart County, Tenn., who died in 1848, leaving one daughter, now living, named Emily E. January 15, 1850, the Doctor was married to his present wife, Miss Eliza J. Taylor, of Pittsboro, N. C. The following are their children: George T., agent for the Texas Central Railroad at Kaufman, Tex.; Annie Ridgely and Richard H., assistant postmaster at Jackson. The Doctor has been a Democrat in politics since the war, but was originally an old line Whig, and edited the West Tennessee *Whig* two years during 1850 and 1852. He also owned an interest in the paper. He is an ancient I. O. O. F. and Mason, and member of the G. R. Himself and wife are members of the Methodist Episcopal Church South, with which he has been connected thirty-eight years.

R. M. Davis, an old prominent pioneer citizen of Madison County, was born November 5, 1823, in Halifax County, Va., and is one of eleven children born to Samuel and Susan (Caldwell) Davis, our subject and one brother, Samuel C., now a resident of Claiborne County, Ark., being the surviving members. The paternal grandfather was a native of Ireland, but came to America at the commencement of the Revolutionary war, serving throughout the same. The maternal grandparents were born in Virginia, the nativity of our subject's parents also, where they were married and followed agricultural pursuits until 1833, at which date they came to Madison County and located on the farm where our subject has ever since resided, about two miles southwest of Pinson, containing 300 acres. The mother's death occurred in 1859, and the father's in 1863. Our subject has always farmed, and remained with his parents during their lifetime. In December, 1842, he married Sarah Vantrice, native of Smith County, Tenn., where she was born October 1, 1821. To this union have been born Samuel V., James H., Wm. Clarke, Richard M., Peter C., Benj. F. (now living), and John T., Jos. C., and Sarah F., deceased. The children now living are all married but one, three living in this county and three in Arkansas, all farmers. Subject and family are members of the Methodist Church, and five of his sons are with him identified with the F. & A. M., and all are identified with the Democratic party.

Joseph H. Day was born in Madison County, Tenn., in 1849. He is the son of George W. and Sarah (Wilson) Day, who were born in Virginia and Mississippi, respectively. George W. Day was a Baptist divine, and was engaged in ministerial labors for forty-three years. He died in Madison County in 1879, being in his seventy-sixth year. His mother died in 1856, about thirty-six years of age. The father was married three times, the subject being a son of the second wife. Our subject was reared in Madison County, and for the last six years has been engaged in the hotel business in Jackson. In the year 1872 he married Mattie E. Burgess, daughter of Abram Curtis and Nannie (Hudson) Burgess. She was born in North Carolina in 1855, and came to Tennessee in 1868. Her parents were natives of North Carolina, and reared a family of four children. He died in 1880. Mr. and Mrs. Day became the parents of one child, named Clarence Curtis, who died at the age of three years. Mrs. Day is a member of the Baptist Church. Mr. Day is a Democrat in politics.

Capt. William D. Deupree was born in Noxubee County, Miss., May 22, 1834; son of Dr. Elijah and Eliza M. (Wayne) Deupree, natives of Oglethorpe County, Ga. William D. was reared to manhood in his native State and county, and was educated at Union University, Murfreesboro, Tenn. He followed agriculture in Mississippi until the breaking out of the war, when he enlisted in Noxubee Cavalry, First Mississippi Regiment, and served as sergeant until 1863, when he was promoted to a captaincy in the Sixteenth Confederate Regiment, and served thus until the close of the war. He then resumed the management of his plantation, and followed merchandising in his native place until 1874, when he came to Jackson and began dealing in cotton. He has continued that occupation up to the present time, and has met with good success. He still retains his farm in Mississippi. In 1860 he married Miss Emma E. Bush, of Mobile, Ala., and by her is the father of three children: Willie A., a daughter and two sons—Albert B. and Thomas C. Mr. Deupree is a Democrat, but previous to the war was an old line Whig. He is a Mason, Knights Templar degree, and belongs to the K. of P. He and family are Baptists in their religious belief.

John Donnell, a worthy citizen of the Twelfth District, was born in North Carolina in 1824, and is the son of John and Jane S. (McGaha) Donnell. The parents are natives of North Carolina, and came to Tennessee in 1835, and located in this county. The father was a life-long farmer, and accumulated considerable property. He and wife were members of the Presbyterian Church. He was born in 1789 and died in 1882. His wife was born in 1790, and died about 1869. Our subject was reared on a farm, and has followed it all his life, being very prosperous. In 1846 he married Miss Adaline Barham, of Carroll County. She was born in Madison County, Tenn., in 1826, and is the mother of three children—one daughter and two sons. One son died in infancy. His wife died in 1853. He has a good farm of 280 acres, that is well improved. He is a member of the Presbyterian Church, and also of the Masonic order. In politics he is a Democrat.

George W. Donnell was born in North Carolina, in 1826, and is the son of John and Jane S. (McGaha) Donnell, both parents being natives of the above named State. They came to Tennessee in 1835, locating in this county, and were farmers by occupation, acquiring a considerable competency. Both were members of the Presbyterian Church. The father was born in 1789 and died in 1882. The mother was born in 1790, and died in 1869. They were excellent people. Our subject has spent his life thus far on a farm. In 1859 he married Josephine Ellis, daughter of John W. and M. (Norval) Ellis, who was born in Marshall County, Miss., in 1838, and is the mother of four sons and four daughters. Both parents were members of the old school Presbyterian Church. Mr. Donnell is a member of the Masonic order, and is a Democrat. A portion of his present well improved farm he inherited from his father. Mr. Donnell is one of the substantial citizens of the county.

Thomas H. Drake was born in Carroll County, Tenn., December 17, 1835. His father, Dr. James W. Drake, was born in Virginia, in 1803 and came to Tennessee about 1833, locating in Carroll County. Here he farmed and practiced his profession the remainder of his life. He was married in Carroll County to Margaret Woods, daughter of John Woods, a farmer and native of Kentucky. The fruits of their union were seven children, our subject being the eldest and the only living member of the family. Dr. Drake died in 1877, and his wife, who was born in Giles County, Tenn., in 1808, died at the old homestead in 1865. Thomas H. Drake received his preparatory education at Spring Creek, Tenn., and graduated from Center College at Danville, Ky. He spent ten years as a teacher, has practiced law and is now giving his attention to farming. He served in the Twelfth Tennessee Infantry under Col. Russell, and was in the battle of Belmont, Mo., and other engagements. He was married in Jackson, Tenn., November 12, 1867, to Louisa Miller, daughter of John S. Miller, a retired merchant. The following are their children: John M., Sarah P., Clifford C. and Alice A. Mrs. Drake was born in Bolivar, Tenn., March 29, 1845, and Mr. Drake is a Democrat and Mason, and he and Mrs. Drake are members of the Presbyterian Church. Their farm, consisting of 189 acres of land, is situated about four and a half miles north of Jackson.

Adrian D. Dugger, merchant of Jackson, Tenn., was born in Petersburg, Va., February 14, 1845, son of William and Sarah (Foster) Dugger, both natives of Virginia. The father removed to Panola County, Miss., in 1848, where our subject was raised and educated. Upon the breaking out of the war he enlisted in Company C, Twenty-ninth Regiment Mississippi Infantry, participating in twenty-three battles, and was slightly wounded five times. After the war he engaged in mercantile business in Mississippi, and accepted still later the position of deputy circuit clerk and deputy sheriff of Panola County, Miss., and in 1874 came to Jackson and engaged as clerk and book-keeper in a mercantile business, and in 1878 returned to Mississippi, but in 1880 again returned here and engaged in the grocery business, in which he has continued until the present time, having met with good and well deserved success, and carries the largest and best selected stock of groceries in the city and county, and commands the leading trade in his line. In 1878 Mr. Dugger married Miss Sallie T. Hall, daughter of R. W. Hall, of this city; they have two sons living. He is a Democrat, Mason and a member of the I. O. O. F., K. of H., K. of G. R., A. O. U. W., and a member of the Methodist Episcopal Church.

Hon. B. A. Enloe was born in Carroll County, Tenn., near the village of Clarksburg, January 18, 1848. He is the son of B. S. Enloe, a native of Tennessee, and Nancy O. (Blair) Enloe, of North Carolina. He was educated at Bethel College and Cumberland University, graduating from the law department of the latter institution in January, 1873. He was elected to the Legislature from Carroll County as a Democrat, in 1869, taking his seat soon after he attained his majority, and was re-elected in 1870. In 1872 he was delegate to the National Democratic Convention at Baltimore. He commenced the practice of law at Nashville, in 1873, but soon came to Jackson to enter the law firm of Brown, Enloe & Bullock. In October, 1874, he and Robert Gates purchased the *Courier-Herald*, and established the *Jackson Sun*, which was consolidated with the *Whig and Tribune* in 1877, under the name of the *Tribune and Sun*, and Mr. Enloe has been editor and proprietor of the latter journal almost continuously since that time. In 1876 he was the Tilden and Hendricks elector for the Eighth District, and he served on the State executive committee from 1878 to 1880. He was appointed commissioner in company with N. Baxter, Jr., by Gov. Marks, in 1879, to negotiate a settlement of the State debt at 50-4. He presided over the State Convention in 1880, and was made a delegate to the National Democratic Convention at Cincinnati. In 1886 he was elected to Congress as a representative from the Eighth District, over the Hon. Sam. W. Hawkins, the Republican nominee, by a majority of 1,697 votes. Mr. Enloe is a member of the Masonic, Odd Fellows, and Knights of Pythias fraternities, and a member of the Methodist Episcopal Church South. He married Fannie H. Ashworth, of Wilson County, Tenn., April 5, 1870, and has one son and three daughters living.

Louis Eppinger, a well-to-do citizen of Jackson, was born in the Kingdom of Wurtemberg, Germany, February 6, 1838, and came to the United States in 1851. He learned the barber's trade in Philadelphia, and worked there and at New York City, until 1858, when he came to Jackson and established a shop here, which he has run successfully ever since, having the only first-class barber shop in the city. In 1861 he married Miss Margaret Wittman, who died in 1873, leaving two living children: John F. and Louis W. Mr. Eppinger is Democratic in politics, is a Mason and K. of L. He has been very successful in business, owning the property in which he does business, and is also owner of two good residences, and in 1886 erected a large two-story brick building on the corner of Market and College Streets, which is used as a K. of L. hall above; and his son, John F., uses the first floor, in which he conducts a first-class bakery and confectionery.

Emanuel Felsenthal, one of the prominent grocers of this city, was born in Germany, in 1845, and came to the United States in 1860, and located in Brownsville, Tenn., and engaged in the grocery business, which he continued for ten years. In 1883 he came to this city and engaged in the grocery business, and by industry and fair dealing has commanded a fair trade. In 1872 he was united in marriage to Miss Carrie Anker, daughter of Seligman and Jennet Anker. She was born in Brownsville, Tenn., in 1856, and is the mother of seven children—four females and three males. He and wife are members of the Jewish temple at Brownsville. Mr. Felsenthal began life without any assistance from parents or friends, working hard and earning his own money. He is a member of the following orders: Masonic, K. of P. and K. of H.

Burkett & Fletcher are wholesale and retail grocers of Jackson, Tenn., and the firm is composed of J. W. N. Burkett and R. S. Fletcher. They began business on the 3d of January, 1883, with a capital stock of $7,000, which they have since increased to $10,000. They do quite a large wholesale business with neighboring towns in Henderson, Carroll and Chester Counties, and command a large share of the retail trade in the town and county. Robert S. Fletcher was born in Madison County, Tenn., May 13, 1849, son of John T. and Caroline (Compton) Fletcher, natives respectively, of North Carolina and Virginia. Robert S. was educated at Clayton's Creek College, Ky., and Andrew College, of Trenton, Tenn. He taught school in Madison and Fayette Counties for about six years, and in 1878 accepted the position as editor of the Jackson *Dispatch*, editing the same about one year. He then leased the paper for two years and purchased a one-half interest in the West Tennessee *Whig*. In 1883 he engaged in the grocery business and has met with well deserved success. October 3, 1884, he married Matie Walker, of Brownsville, Tenn., who died September 17, 1885, leaving one son—Robert Savage. January 14, 1886, Mr. Fletcher wedded his present wife, Pattie C. Walker. He is a Democrat and an ardent worker for his party. He is also a Mason and a thoroughly honorable business man.

F. J. Fly was born in Nashville, Tenn., December 7, 1830, and is the son of Micager and Loretta (Lowe) Fly, both natives of this State. The father was a farmer in early life, but later became a Baptist minister. He came to Madison County about 1834, and lived here until his death, in 1865. His wife died in 1846, after having borne a family of ten children. The father's second wife was Mrs. Frances Senter, widow of James Senter. She died in 1880. Our subject thus far through life has followed farming as an occupation. In 1852 he wedded Luvina Day, of this county, daughter of Lemuel and Mary (Senter) Day, who was born in this State in 1834, and is the mother of five sons and one daughter. This lady died in 1877, and in 1878 he married her half sister, Sarah E. Day, by whom he had three children—two sons and one daughter. His second wife was born in 1853. He and wife are members of the Baptist

Church. He is a Mason, a member of the Agricultural Wheel, and a Democrat. He moved to his present farm in 1865, and in 1872 erected a cotton-gin, which he conducts profitably.

John H. Freeling, farmer, was born in Madison County, Tenn., October 10, 1826. His father, J. H. Freeling, was born in New Jersey, but was reared in North Carolina. He was married in the latter State to Lucy Holmes, and by her became the father of five sons and five daughters—our subject being the seventh member of the family. The father was a prominent and wealthy citizen, and for some time was sheriff of Rowan County, N. C. He came to Tennessee in 1825, and settled in Madison County. He was a farmer, and died in 1843. His wife died in Hardeman County in 1880. Their son, John H., received a common school education, and has followed farming through life. He served a short time in the Confederate Army as a member of Col. Wilson's cavalry, but was discharged for disability. He was married in Madison County, February 3, 1847, to Miss Nancy Carrington, and by her became the father of two sons, John W. and Joseph S., who are practicing physicians: the former at McNairy Station, and the latter at Benton, Mo. Mrs. Freeling was born near Nashville, in 1827, and died at the homestead in Madison County November 4, 1870. Mrs. Julia Exum became Mr. Freeling's second wife. She was born in Arkansas, January 3, 1844, and is a daughter of John F. Wilson, and by Mr. Freeling became the mother of one son, Charles Henry. One son was born to her marriage with Mr. Exum, John R., who is attending college at Jackson. Mr. Freeling is a Mason, and he and wife are members of the Cumberland Presbyterian Church. He owns 450 acres of land, 320 being in the home place.

Julius Friedlob, a prominent dry goods merchant of this city, was born in Poland in 1841, and is the son of L. and Sarah Friedlob. In 1862 he emigrated to the United States, and lived in New York, peddling from that place about six months; then went to St. Louis, following the same business for about nine months; then went to Memphis, where he remained until the day after Lee surrendered; then he came to this city and engaged in the dry goods and clothing business, which has proven very successful. Mr. Friedlob began life poor, his possessions being gained by his own honesty, industry, and perseverance. He occupies his own house, and has other property also in a very desirable portion of the city. In 1868 he was united in marriage to Miss Bettie Felsenthal, daughter of Eli Felsenthal. She was born in Bavaria, Germany, and is the mother of six boys. He is a member of the I. O. O. F., K. of P., K. of H., A. O. U. W., and belongs to a Jewish society in Memphis, called the I. O. B. B., and belongs to the Jewish congregations both here and at Brownsville, Tenn. In politics he is neutral, but Democratic.

Samuel F. Gillikin, grocery merchant, of Jackson, Tenn., was a native of Henderson County, Tenn., born December 9, 1856, son of James and Lucinda (Duncan) Gillikin, natives of North Carolina. Samuel F. was reared on a farm in this county; entered the employ of Illinois Central Railroad, working as a carpenter, fireman and brakeman for that corporation. In 1881 he came to Jackson; September, 1884, engaged in present grocery business, in which he has met with good and well deserved success, carrying now a full and select line of staple and fancy groceries and country produce, and controlling a fair city trade and first-class country trade. Mr. Gillikin is a Democrat in politics; is unmarried, and recognized as one among the successful and enterprising business men of Jackson.

Capt. J. C. Gooch was born in Carroll County, Tenn., May 26, 1842, son of Rowland Gooch, who was born in North Carolina in 1797. After attaining his majority, the father married Hannah Cozart, also of North Carolina. In 1822 he came to Tennessee, locating in Maury County, and became the father of five sons and seven daughters, our subject being the youngest of the family. Rowland Gooch was a farmer and died at his home in Madison County (where he located in 1866) in December, 1873. His widow died at the home of her daughter, Mrs. Howard, in July, 1883. J. C. Gooch attended school until nineteen years of age; then joined the Confederate Army and went out as second lieutenant of Company I, Twenty-seventh Tennessee Infantry, under Col. Kit Williams. He was elected first lieutenant after the battle of Shiloh, but in the latter part of 1862 was discharged on account of disability, and was authorized to raise a company of cavalry. He became captain of the company, and joined Forrest's command in 1863. He participated in many hotly contested battles, and was surrendered at Gainesville, Ala., in 1865. February 24, 1869, he wedded Cordelia R. White, daughter of A. M. White, a farmer and cotton merchant. To Mr. and Mrs. Gooch were born the following children: Arthur M. (deceased October 1, 1878,), Hattie L., George R. and James T., born February 8, 1870; March 17, 1872; April 18, 1874, and January 19, 1876, respectively. Mrs. Gooch was born in Maury County, Tenn., August 6, 1849. Mr. Gooch is a Democrat, and he and wife are members of the Missionary Baptist Church. He owns 546 acres of land, and gives his chief attention to cotton raising.

Rufus C. Gooch, farmer, was born in Carroll County, Tenn., September 2, 1830. [For history of parents, see sketch of Capt. J. C. Gooch.]

He was reared on a farm and received a common school education. He was married in Henderson County, Tenn., February 20, 1856, to Elizabeth C. Gordon, daughter of W. W. Gordon, farmer, and native of West Point, Va. The following are Mr. and Mrs. Gooch's children: Angus, born November 20, 1856; Florence E., born February 22, 1859; S. P. (deceased January 9, 1876), born November 15, 1863; Eva E., born October 22, 1875, and Eunice, born March 6, 1879. Mrs. Gooch was born in Henderson County, Tenn., November 16, 1837. Mr. Gooch served in the late war in the Twelfth Tennessee Cavalry, under Col. Wilson, and was at Brice's Cross Roads, Harrisburg, and was with Forrest during his first campaign in Tennessee. He was captured once and was paroled. He is a Democrat, and he and wife are members of the Missionary Baptist Church. He owns sixty-five acres of land, and has a pleasant and comfortable home.

Balys E. Gray, a prominent and substantial citizen of this city, was born in Charlotte, N. C., in 1844, and in 1852 went to Holly Springs, Miss., where he was reared to manhood. He is the son of E. D. and Sarah E. (Withers) Gray. The parents are natives of North Carolina. The father was a farmer by occupation, was prosperous in early life, but later met with reverses that incumbered him financially. Five children blessed their union, three of whom are yet living. The father died in Holly Springs in 1856, his widow followed him in 1862. In 1861 our subject enlisted in the Confederate service, Seventeenth Mississippi Regiment, and remained with them until the close of the war. In 1872 he was united in marriage to Miss Anna Davidson, of Holly Springs, and daughter of S. M. and Matilda (Cheatham) Davidson. She was born in Mississippi in 1850, and is the mother of four children, three of whom are yet living. In 1874 he moved to this city and engaged in the liquor trade, and continues it up to the present time. Mr. Gray began life poor, his possessions being gained by his own honesty, energy and perseverance. His politics are strictly Democratic. His wife and family are members of the Episcopal Church.

James N. Greer is a native of Lincoln County, this State, his birth occurring December 15, 1818. His father was a North Carolinian and came to Tennessee when a young man, locating in Lincoln County. Here he married Delia McElroy, daughter of Thomas McElroy, a farmer, and to this marriage were born seven sons and four daughters, James N. being the third child. In 1822 the father moved to West Tennessee, which was then very sparsely inhabited, and settled in Madison County. He had previously explored and surveyed much of the surrounding country on a former visit. He followed farming for a livelihood, and died in 1845. The mother was a North Carolinian, and was an exemplary woman. Her death occurred in 1868. James N. is also a farmer, and has been quite successful. September 15, 1858, he was united in marriage with Miss Henrietta, daughter of Augustus Askew, and to this union the following children have been born: Delia E., Robert L., Henrietta E., Virginia C. and Neophlet A. and two that died. The mother was born November 27, 1834, and died December 18, 1880. Mr. Greer is a Democrat, and voted for Henry Clay for President. He opposed secession, but finally went with his State. He owns over 600 acres of land at Oakfield Station, seven miles from Jackson. He is comfortably located, and is a good citizen.

John A. Greer, of this city, was born in Tennessee in 1827, and is the son of Alexander and Margaret (Spratt) Greer. The parents are natives of Mechlenburg County, N. C., and came to Tennessee in 1819. He lived in different counties until 1822, when he moved to Madison. He was a prosperous farmer and owned considerable real estate and slaves. Nine children were born to their union, six of whom lived to become grown, and two only are living at present. The mother died in 1841, the father following in death in 1858. Our subject spent his boyhood days on the farm, and received his education in the common country schools. At the age of seventeen he came to this city and spent two years clerking for Childs & Person; then, on account of ill health, returned to his father's farm, and after a vacation of about one year, he took a trip West, spending three months, and returned to receive a gift of 1,000 acres of land from his father, in the southwestern portion of the county, which he at once located on, remaining until 1854, when he began merchandising in the village of Denmark, this county, and continued until 1859, when he married and returned to his farm. His bride, Miss Louisa Ingram, was born in 1832, and is the daughter of Dr. John and Lydia (McMillan) Ingram. He remained on the farm until 1871, and then moved to this city, yet retaining possession and control of his farm. He is one of the directors in the First National Bank. He and wife are members of the Presbyterian Church. He is a member of the Masonic order, and also of the K. of T. In politics he is strictly Democratic.

Andrew J. Guinn was born in Alabama July 22, 1820, son of John Guinn, who was born in Middle Tennessee, and on attaining his majority married Polly Stewart, a native of Alabama. He was a soldier in the war of 1812, and was at the battle of New Orleans. The family resided in southern Alabama, but a short time prior to 1828 moved to the northern portion of the State and settled near Florence. At the age of eight years our subject ran away from his father and came to Henderson County, where he lived until the second year of the war. In March of that year he moved to Madison County, and settled on his present home farm. He was married in Perry County, June 10, 1840, to Elizabeth Condor, daughter of Daniel Condor, farmer and native of Kentucky. Mr. and Mrs. Guinn's marriage resulted in the birth of thirteen children— four sons and nine daughters. Mrs. Guinn was born in Decatur County January 2, 1825, and is still living. Our subject is a stanch Republican and takes pleasure in the success of his party. He aids in all laudable enterprises, so far as his means will justify, and is well respected by his neighbors and friends. He owns 800 acres of exceptionally fertile land, which he devotes chiefly to the cultivation of cotton. He also owns valuable property in the city of Jackson, and is well and favorably known by the business men of that place.

Joseph D. Hackney was born in North Carolina in 1836, and is the son of James and Keziah (Davis) Hackney, both natives of the same State. They came to Tennessee in 1836, and soon afterward located in this county. The father was a farmer, and himself and wife were the parents of three children, one of whom is dead. The father died in May, 1864, and his wife five years earlier. Joseph D. grew to mature years on a farm, and has since followed farming as an occupation. The drug business, in which he once engaged, was soon abandoned. In 1862 he enlisted in the Confederate Army, and served in the quartermaster's department until the cessation of hostilities, reaching home in May, 1865. In 1855 he married Malinda Pirtle, who was born in 1834 and died in 1879. In 1880 he married Mrs. Mary (Fogg) Barnett, widow of S. A. Barnett. By her first husband she had two children, one of whom, Hattie, is yet living. Mrs. Hackney was born in 1839, and is the daughter of Joseph and Eliza (Madden) Fogg. Her father is a native of Virginia, and came to Tennessee when seventeen years of age. He was twice married, and is the father of thirteen children, three of his boys serving in the Confederate service. Mr. Hackney is a Democrat, and was a useful citizen.

Richard H. Hammerly, general manager and stockholder of the Jackson Milling & Manufacturing Company, was born in Tennessee in 1844; is the son of Joseph and Virginia B. (Noel) Hammerly. Richard H. was reared to manhood in Huntingdon, Carroll Co., Tenn., and received his education in the best schools of that place. In 1862 he enlisted in the Twelfth Kentucky Cavalry, and participated in many of the battles up to March 24, 1864, when he received a gun-shot wound in the right knee, and was totally unfitted for further service. He located in

Jackson in October, 1864, and he and his father engaged in the livery business. They afterward became coal and lumber merchants, and then began selling beer and ice. In December, 1885, he purchased an interest in his present business and became manager of the same. In 1880 he was married to Ada F. Flack, of Memphis, Tenn., daughter of Sanders Flack. Mr. and Mrs. Hammerly have two daughters and one son. Himself and wife are members of the First Methodist Church, and he is a Democrat in his political views and has been a successful business man and is highly respected and esteemed.

Miles M. Hammond, a grocer of this city, was born in South Carolina in 1820, and came to Tennessee with his parents in 1829. He is the son of William and Elizabeth R. (Morgan) (Powell) Hammond. His father farmed in early life, and afterward engaged in the manufacture of wagons. He departed this life in 1874, his wife dying in 1843. The father married for his second wife a Miss Hern. His third wife is yet living. Our subject was reared to early manhood on the farm, and educated in the country schools. At the age of eighteen he began learning the blacksmith trade at Parker's Cross roads, remaining there about two years; then came to this city, and in partnership with Abner Teague ran a shop, afterward taking John H. Day as a partner. After engaging in the blacksmith business about twelve years, our subject was superseded by his brother. He next engaged in the tinware and hardware business, which he conducted for about one year; then engaged in the family grocery business, shortly afterward adding dry goods, which business he ran successfully until the breaking out of the war, when, owing to the financial depression, he suspended business until the close of the war, then opened again and was doing a thriving business up to 1875, when his stock was consumed by fire, sustaining a heavy loss. In the fall of the same year he engaged as silent partner in the well known grocery house of W. & D. Hopper, remaining for two and one-half years; then engaged in the same business alone, and was again burned out in 1882; but in the fall of the same year he began business again and continued up to the present time. In 1853 he married Miss Margaret Simington. She was born in Tennessee in 1832, and is the mother of eight children, five of whom are living: Maude C., married to James Medlin, and after his death married to D. R. Staley; Iva R., married to Wm. Dodds; Walter, James and Leigh. His wife is a member of the old school Presbyterian Church, and in politics he is Democratic.

Jesse H. Harper, a prominent gun and clock smith of this city, was born in North Carolina, in 1826, and is the son of Edward and Martha (Hancock) Harper. The parents were natives of North Carolina. The father was an artisan and farmer, being very successful through life. He had a family of eleven children. Three of his sons became merchants, and one a Baptist minister. The father was not a member of the church, yet his house was ever open for all ministers. The father supported a widowed mother and nine children, and at the age of twenty-two erected a house in which he lived until his death, which occurred in 1857. His widow followed him in 1876. Our subject lived to the age of fifteen years on his father's farm, and then entered the academy of Pittsboro, remaining two years, then spent some years in different schools, the latter portion of which he was partly pupil and partly assistant teacher. He taught school two years at Montezuma, Tenn., and two years at Mifflin, and two years at Shady Grove Academy, near Jackson. In 1852 he was married to Sarah E., daughter of James Henderson, ex-trustee of this county. She was born in this State, in 1832, and is the mother of five children—three daughters and two sons. The oldest daughter is dead. After marriage he moved to Haywood County and taught school at Alamo, remaining some time, then moved to this city. He taught school at Cerro Gordo, this county, for one year, then purchased property and erected a residence, which is known as Harper's Male and Female Institute. Since locating in this city he has taught an army of children, numbering over 3,000. The doors of his school are thrown open for the rich and poor alike. In 1855 he was elected alderman of this city, and afterward served as tax collector, and in 1860 served as mayor of the city; was defeated in 1861 for same office on account of his politics, he being a Union man. During the years from 1866 to 1868 he was postmaster, and elected by the Legislature to the land register office in West Tennessee, and was one of the three commissioners appointed for Madison County; was elected city recorder, and held the office of justice of the peace. In 1870 he was appointed mail agent on the Mississippi Central Railroad, holding that office two years. Mr. Harper is a self-made man and possesses many rare accomplishments. He and wife are members of the First Methodist Church, and he is a member of the I. O. O. F. and also of that honorable order called Free and Accepted Masons. He is the eternal foe of ignorance and therefore has a poor regard for any man who opposes national education. He built his own institute, at his own expense, and gave poor children more than $20,000 in tuition, books, slates, pencils, food, clothing, etc. He hopes that he may be permitted to live until education is the common birthright of every child, who shall have every right in law that man may claim for himself. The following is one of his hand-bills published thirty years ago. It says: "True education is the only guide to happiness. We believe that education is the common birthright of every child of man, and that the legislator who refuses his influence to perfect the title to this greatest of all human rights, is simply a disgrace to the position he occupies, and a robber of the rising generation of its brightest jewel, which is liberty to know the truth. Send the children to the Jackson Male and Female Institute, and they will be received and properly educated; and to the poor and needy and to those who have no money we say: 'Come.'"

Julius C. Harris is a Rowan County North Carolinian, born February 21, 1822. His father, Wesley Harris, was born in Montgomery County, N. C., and came to Tennessee in 1831, where he afterward followed farming. He was married to Mary R. Barringer, who was born also in North Carolina, and they became the parents of eight sons and two daughters. The father died in 1861, and the mother in 1863. Julius C. Harris is the eldest of his father's family, and after attending the common schools he enlisted in the Confederate Army and served for a period of one year, when he was discharged from the service for over age. November 18, 1852, he married Susan C. Smith, daughter of James S. Smith, and their union resulted in the birth of one son— Walter S., born February 12, 1858. The mother died in 1858, and March 3, 1859, Mr. Harris married Martha King, daughter of B. T. King, a merchant. Mr. and Mrs. Harris have two children: Edward W. and Mary S. (Mrs. Smith). The mother was born in Williamson County, Tenn., November 30, 1839. Mr. Harris is a Democrat and has served his district as magistrate for many years. He devotes his farm, which consists of 875 acres, to raising grain, cotton and stock.

Walter S. Harris is a Madison County Tennessean, born February 12, 1858, the only child of Julius C. and Susan C. (Smith) Harris, and is of Irish descent. [For history of his parents, see biography of J. C. Harris.] Walter S. spent his boyhood days in working on the farm and attending school. When twenty-three years old he began doing for himself, and by industry and economy owns 255 acres of land, on which he raises cotton, principally. He was married in Madison County, December 20, 1882, to Lizzie W. Glenn, daughter of Dr. James R. Glenn, who was born in North Carolina, March 30, 1800, and died in Jackson, Tenn., August 30, 1881. His wife was born in North Carolina in 1822, and is still living in Madison County. Mrs. Harris was born in Madison County, Tenn., March 17, 1860; Mr. Harris is a Democrat and his first presidential vote was cast for Gen. Hancock.

Benjamin R. Harris, M. D., was born in Orange County, N. C., February 5, 1825, and is the son of William and Maria W. (Briggs) Harris. The parents are natives respectively of North Carolina and Virginia.

The father moved to Maury County in 1834, spending his early life in the pulpit, later engaging in farming. He died in January, 1856, the mother following in death in 1873. Our subject attended school in the county of his birth; he being the oldest child, the care of his father's family fell almost entirely upon him, which deprived him of many advantages of school. He lived on the farm until twenty-four years of age, when he began reading medicine, attending his first course in 1851–52, and graduated in the medical department of the University at Nashville in 1853. He then located at Purdy, McNairy County, and began the practice of his profession, remaining twelve years, then located in this city, and has done a large remunerative practice. Since locating in this city, he has been engaged in the family grocery and real estate business. In 1861 he was united in marriage to Miss Ellen Anderson, of McNairy County, and daughter of William T. and Mahala (Wisdom) Anderson. She (the wife) was born in Tennessee in 1837. Five children have blessed this union, three sons and two daughters, all of whom yet remain under the parental roof. He is a member of the Methodist Church, and his wife, one son and one daughter are members of the Cumberland Presbyterian Church. He is a member of the Masonic order, and in politics he is a Democrat. He is Past Grand Master of the F. & A. M., and has reached the thirty-third degree of Scottish Rite.

Hon. Robert W. Haynes, attorney at law of Jackson, Tenn., was born in Washington County, Tenn., August 21, 1840, son of Landon C. and Eleanor M. (Powell) Haynes, both natives of Tennessee. [See sketch elsewhere of father.] Robert., subject of this sketch, was reared to manhood in his native county, attending Emory and Henry College, Virginia, three years. He then entered the university of North Carolina, from which institution he graduated after a two years' course (in 1862). In the meantime, upon the breaking out of the war, he entered the Confederate service in 1861, serving under Maj. Glover, until failing health compelled him to leave the service, and he then returned to school and graduated. After his graduation he re-entered service, and assisted in raising a company for Col. Fain's regiment, but served as *aide* on the staff of Col. James E. Rains, Eleventh Tennessee, commanding brigade of Stevenson's division, Gen. Kirby Smith's corps, serving thus in Bragg's Kentucky campaign. He then served as adjutant of the Sixty-second North Carolina Infantry, until 1863, when he accepted the position of *aide* to Brig.-Gen. Alfred E. Jackson, serving thus with the rank of first lieutenant until the surrender, being brevetted near the close to major, and appointed assistant adjutant-general on the staff of Maj.-Gen. John C. Vaughan, having been virtually raised in a law office. Mr. Haynes, after the war, perfected his knowledge of his profession, and in April, 1867, commenced the practice of law at Memphis with his father, and continued thus successfully until 1870, when he removed to Jackson, where he has since practiced. January 12, 1863, he was married, in Knoxville, Tenn., to Miss Drusie Powell, of Virginia. They have five children: Nellie, Landon C. (a girl), Robert P., Walter L. and Drusie Taylor. Mr. Haynes is and always has been an unswerving Democrat in political views. He represented Madison County in the State Legislature, serving two terms successively in the sessions of 1883 and 1885. He is a Knight Templar Mason, and is a member of the K. of P., K. of H., and K. of G. R., being one of the founders of the latter order, and Past Supreme Commander and Secretary of same. Himself and wife are members of the Methodist Episcopal Church South, in which he has been an official for eighteen years, and for many years represented the district conference, being at present secretary of same. He has served for the past four years as lay delegate in the Memphis Annual Conference, and as secretary of the board of missions of the conference. He was elected at the Paducah Conference, in December, 1885, one of the alternate delegates to the general conference of the church. He is also president of the West Tennessee Sunday-school Convention, and is one of the present delegates to the International Sunday-school Convention, which will meet in Chicago in May, 1887.

Stokely D. Hays, attorney at law, is the son of Richard J. and Sarah A. (Ballou) Hays, and was born in this county April 4, 1852. His father, who is an eminent lawyer of this city, came to this county from Davidson County at an early day. Stokely D. was educated in this county, and early in life began the study of law. He was for a few years deputy clerk of the supreme court, and was for a short time clerk of the supreme court of Tennessee at Jackson. After the expiration of his early official positions he began the practice of law here, and has since been thus engaged, having met with merited success. In June, 1884, he formed a partnership with John A. Pitts, and in June, 1886, Gen. Meeks became a partner of the firm. May 18, 1876, Mr. Hays was united in marriage with Gertrude Stovall, of Fulton County, Ky., and to this union there are two living children: Katie S. and Sarah B. Mr. Hays is a Democrat, a member of the K. of H., and himself and wife are members of the Methodist Episcopal Church South, and for many years he was superintendent of the first Methodist Episcopal Sunday-school at Jackson. He was the chairman of the building committee, which erected the present beautiful church at Jackson, said to be the most artistic in the South.

Uriah R. Heavner, a contractor of this city, was born in North Carolina in 1847, and is the son of Teater and Elizabeth Heavner, who are also natives of North Carolina. The father was a mechanic by trade, and died in 1885. The parents had nine children born to their union, four of whom are still living. At the age of twenty our subject went to Mississippi, and in 1872 married Miss Sue Long, of Paris, Tenn., and daughter of Antony Long. She was born in Kentucky about 1848, and is the mother of two children—Reuben and Maggie. In 1875 he came to this city, and has been engaged in carpentering and contracting up to the present time, and is a first-class architect. His wife is a member of the Methodist Church and he of the Baptist. He is a Democrat and member of the Masonic order.

J. P. Hendrix, proprietor of the grocery department of the State Wheel Store at Jackson, was born March 7, 1855, in Henderson County, Tenn., and is of a family of three sons and five daughters, born to R. L. and Mary (Grider) Hendrix, of which our subject and four sisters are the surviving members. The parents were born in South Carolina and married in Henderson County, Tenn., where they farmed till their deaths, 1865 and 1875, mother and father respectively. After the mother's death the father married Miss Emeline Allen, whose death occurred in 1885. Our subject remained at home till he was sixteen, since which time he has held clerkships for various mercantile firms of Jackson until the fall of 1886, when he took charge of the grocery department of the Jackson store for the State Wheel. Their stock consists of general groceries to the amount of about $3,000. October 24, 1882, he married Miss Sally H. Taylor, a native of Jackson, to whom one son and one daughter, both still living, have been born: John P. and Mary Theodocia. Mrs. Hendrix is a member of the Episcopal Church, and he of the I. O. O. F. and K. of H. Politically he is a Democrat.

Ransom B. Hicks, a prominent farmer, was born within two miles of Jackson, Tenn., June 12, 1839. He was the ninth of ten sons born to George and Joyce Ella (Kirby) Hicks. George Hicks was born in Sussex County, Va., September 10, 1796, and came to Tennessee when a young man. He settled in Robertson County, where he married, and in 1822 moved to Madison County, where he spent the remainder of his days. He was a man of energy and perseverance, and honesty and integrity were his guiding stars. He succeeded in accumulating considerable of this world's goods, and placed all his sons in respectable and prosperous positions in life. He died at the home of his son, Kenneth B. Hicks, near Jackson, Tenn., on Friday, February 1, 1878. His wife was born in Robertson County, Tenn., and died at Springfield while on a visit to her native county. Ransom B. Hicks was educated in the common schools, and on the 9th of October, 1861, wedded Lydia C. Withers, daughter of Radford Withers, a farmer and native North Carolinian. Mr. and Mrs. Hicks became the parents of three sons and one daughter, Johnnie Bob and George Ransom being the only ones now living. Mrs. Hicks was born in Madison County November 17, 1838. Her father died at his home in this county April 27, 1869, and her mother January 2, 1870. Mr. Hicks is a Democrat, a Mason and a K. of P., and he, his wife and oldest son are members of the Missionary Baptist Church. He served throughout the late war in the Fifty-first Tennessee Infantry under Col. Chester. He owns 530 acres of land, which is devoted to the raising of cotton, the cereals and stock.

Hill, Stedman & Co. are one of the substantial business houses of Jackson. Samuel B. Hill, of this company, was born in this county, in 1862, son of Robert N. and E. A. (Maxey) Hill. The father was a native of the Emerald Isle, and came to Tennessee in 1842, engaging in the cotton commission business at Perryville, and later in mercantile pursuits at Spring Creek, continuing until 1873, when he retired, and two years later, came to Jackson, where he died in 1884. The mother was a native of Tennessee. S. B. Hill, one of the subjects of this sketch, was educated at Madison College, and in 1875 commenced active work, in the capacity of salesman, until 1886, when the above company was formed. In 1881 he married Lena M. Robbins, a native of Tennessee, born in 1865, and died in 1884, leaving one child, Annie L. Hill. Mr. Hill is a Democrat, and a member of the Cumberland Presbyterian Church. Elisha P. Stedman, of the above firm, was born in Tennessee, in 1852, and is the son of Nathan W. and Sarah (Williamson) Stedman, and the youngest of their twelve children. The parents were born in Chatham County, N. C., and came to Tennessee about 1830. The father was a successful farmer, and died in 1859; the mother died in 1885. Elisha P. passed his youth as a farmer's boy, receiving limited education. In 1881, he came to this city, and with the exception of five months, when he was on the police force, clerked until 1886, when he entered into his present partnership. In November, 1877, he was married to Miss Alice W., daughter of Jacob and Nancy E. (Whitlow) Vanhook, who was born in 1859, and has borne her husband three children: Ernest P., Bertha, and an infant not yet named. Mr. Stedman is a Democrat, a member of the K. of P., and of the Methodist Church, and his firm is one of the most active and successful of this city.

J. H. Hirsch, saddler and dealer in buggies, carriages and hides, was born in November, 1839, in Jefferson County, Ky., and is of a family of seven children, born to Chas. and Catharine Hirsch. The father was born in Germany, the mother in the United States; they were married at Louisville, Ky., where the father practiced veterinary surgery, until his death, about 1850, the mother following in 1866. Our subject remained at home until he was seventeen years old; he then served an apprenticeship of three years at the harness trade, with R. E. Miles of Louisville. He then went to Aberdeen, Miss., plying his trade until the commencement of the war; he then continued his trade in the service of the Confederate Government, until his marriage, in 1863, to Ada B. Kelley, a native of Christian County, Ky. At the close of the war, he moved to Leavenworth, Kas., where he remained a few months, and then moved to Lexington, Mo., where he resided one year; he then made Paducah, Ky., his home for four years; then came to Jackson and established his saddlery and hide trade at the corner of Lafayette and Liberty Streets, where he remained until 1874. He then built the business house he now occupies, on the corner of College and Liberty Streets. He was also engaged in the saddlery trade while in Kansas and Missouri. He has recently added a line of carriages, etc., and carries a stock (including harness stock) of about $2,500. He has bought as high as $10,000 worth of hides in a single year. To the marriage referred to above, four sons and one daughter have been born, the daughter and two sons still living. He and his family are members of the Presbyterian Church, and he is also a member of the I. O. O. F. and K. of H.

Wm. Holland, the popular dry goods merchant of this city, was born in South Carolina. He merchandised in his native State until 1871, when he came to Jackson and resumed the mercantile business here. He is the son of John and Susan (Brockman) Holland. The parents are natives of South Carolina, and died in 1884 and 1873 respectively. In 1868 he was united in marriage to Miss Hattie Sullivan, of South Carolina, daughter of Dr. James Sullivan. She was born in 1847 and is the mother of four children: Edith, Carolina, Willie and John. He, wife and the oldest two children are members of the Methodist Church. He is a member of the K. of P., and in politics he is strictly Democratic. Mr. Holland spent his early life on the farm, and received his education in the common county schools.

Daniel Hopper is the son of James Hopper, and was born in Henry County, Va., May 28, 1812. His father was also a Virginian and followed the occupation of farming through life. His grandfather, William Hopper, was a resident of Virginia and served the colonies in the Revolution. For gallant service he was granted a pension, which continued until his death. The mother of Daniel was Miss Elizabeth Oaks, who married her husband about 1798 and bore him ten sons, of whom only three are now living. Her husband dying during the war of 1812, she came to Tennessee with her family, in 1835, and located in Madison County. About 1852 she went back to Virginia, her native State, but just before the late war moved to North Carolina and there died at the age of eighty years. Daniel was reared a farmer, and has followed that vocation. In 1836 he came to Madison County, and October 4, 1838, was married to Miss Lucinda, daughter of Stephen Burrus. This lady bore him four children, two now living: Susan C. and William M. The mother was born in East Tennessee, February 7, 1823, and two years later was brought to Madison County. Her death occurred here February 5, 1885. Mr. Hopper is a Democrat, a Mason, and owns over 1,300 acres of land, 800 acres of which compose his home farm, six miles northeast of Jackson.

Maj. Erie S. Hosford, agent for the Illinois Central Railroad at Jackson, Tenn., was born in Crawford County, Ohio, August 28, 1834, and is the son of Asa and Alta (Kent) Hosford, natives, respectively, of New York and Pennsylvania. Erie S. Hosford was reared to manhood and educated in his native State. At the age of seventeen he engaged in the railroad business in Ohio, and in December, 1852, came south. In 1853 he accepted the position of civil engineer with the Mobile & Ohio Railway, and served the company in this capacity and as passenger conductor and master of transportation until December, 1865, when he was made division superintendent of the road. He served the company faithfully and efficiently until July 1, 1886. In November, 1886, he entered the employ of the Illinois Central Railroad, at Jackson. In 1859 he married Lucy E. Scales, a native of Tennessee. They have four children living: Walter S., Erie S., Nat. S. and Asa S. Maj. Hosford is and always has been a Democrat in politics; he is a Mason, Knights Templar degree, and is one of the prominent citizens of Jackson.

James J. House, who is engaged in the livery business in Jackson, Tenn., was born in Hall County, Ga., on October 18, 1828. He is one of three surviving members of a family of five children born to Willis and Nancy (Jarrell) House, who were born and married in Oglethorpe County, Ga. They soon moved from Georgia to Marshall County, Miss., where the head of the family was a planter until his death, in August, 1860. His widow, the mother of the subject of this sketch, still survives and resides in Texas. Her son made his parents' home his until the year 1850, when he married Miss Emily Morgan, the youngest daughter of Theophilus and Nancy Morgan nee Mason. Mrs. Emily House's father was a Revolutionary soldier, and a relative of Gen. Daniel Morgan, of Revolutionary fame. He was present at the surrender of Gen. Cornwallis. She was also related to Gen. John Morgan of civil war fame, and a sister of the late lamented W. M. Morgan, of Henderson County, Tenn., who was noted for his piety and unusual worth of character, and as one of the pioneers of Tennessee, sharing cheerfully the privations of the first settlers, while he vindicated the reputation of the State as a good stock country by raising fine horses. Mrs. House has had brothers in every war in this country since that of 1812, one serving at the battle of New Orleans. Her father was a native of North Carolina. Mr. House embarked in the livery and sale business in Holly Springs, Miss., after his marriage, then in November, 1874, removed to Jackson, Tenn., to engage in his present business in livery and stock. During the war he was detailed to purchase horses and other stock for the Confederate Government. He is an active and zealous Democrat, espousing his political cause with great fervor and energy. He is the father of one living child, a daughter, Leonora, the accomplished wife of W. W. Searcy, merchant, of Jackson, Tenn.

Benjamin F. Howard was born in Henderson County, Tenn., February 5, 1826, son of William and Ursula (Hinson) Howard, both natives of Anson County, N. C. The father removed to Tennessee in 1825, where he died in 1858. Benjamin F. was reared on a farm in his native county, and secured a fair English education. After he attained his majority he farmed for himself, and in 1874 came to Jackson and engaged in the livery business, and has continued to the present time. He has a large transfer and drayage business. July 29, 1853, he married Julia F. Timberlake, of Henderson County, and nine living children are the result of their union. Mr. Howard was a Democrat in politics, although he was formerly an old line Whig. In August, 1881, he was elected magistrate of the Fifteenth District, filling the office faithfully to the present. Mr. Howard is one of Jackson's best known and most highly respected citizens, and it is his chief delight in his declining years to entertain his friends by many interesting reminiscences of "ye olden time." Benjamin J. Howard, his son, was born in Henderson County, December 31, 1859, and was reared on a farm. When about twelve years old he was brought to Jackson and was here educated. He was in the livery business with his father until August, 1886, when he was elected to the circuit clerk's office, and has filled the same very efficiently. November 10, 1881, he married Nina E., daughter of Maj. W. D. Robinson. They have three children, Sadie, John W. and Henry. Mr. Howard is one of the representatives of the young Democracy in Madison County, and is a reliable citizen and popular official.

William R. Howlett was born near Nashville, Tenn., April 23, 1819.

His father, Maj. Isaac H. Howlett, was born in East Tennessee, but took up his abode in Middle Tennessee when a young man. He settled in Nashville when it was but a small collection of log cabins. By his proficiency in the military affairs of the State he was given the rank of major. He married Elizabeth M. Ramsey, and our subject is the fourth of their eight children. The father died near Nashville about 1832, and the mother in Madison County in the spring of 1844. William R. received a limited early education, and in October, 1843, married A. E. Dickson, daughter of Robert Dickson. To them were born six children: Sterling G., born February 12, 1848; William J. (deceased), born May 6, 1854; James E. (deceased), born May 23, 1858; Foster B., born May 20, 1862, and Annie Lorena, born September 24, 1866. Mrs. Howlett was born in Madison County, November 5, 1828. Her parents were born in Middle Tennessee, and died at Old Cotton Grove, Tenn., in 1833. William R. Howlett is a Democrat and Mason.

Robert Allen Hurt, clerk and master of the chancery court was born in the city January 3, 1858; son of Robert Bailey and Susan Allen (DeBerry) Hurt, natives of Halifax County, Va., and Madison County, Tenn., respectively. The father came to Carroll County, Tenn., when a boy, about 1830, and six years later located in Madison County. He soon after moved to Nashville, where he clerked in a mercantile and cotton establishment until he was of age, then returned to Madison Co., married and located on a plantation, which he managed successfully the remainder of his life. During the war he was one of Gen. Beauregard's most active aids with the rank of Major. After the war he was a bond and stock broker, and an enterprising citizen of the county. He was instrumental in bringing the I. C. and M. O. Railroads through Jackson. He was a Whig before the war, and in 1859–60 represented his county in the Legislature. In 1875 he was a member of that body as a Democrat. He died August 30, 1881, of cancer, his death being universally regretted throughout the county. Robert A. was reared to manhood in Jackson and Madison Counties. He secured a good education in West Tennessee College, later known as the Southwestern Baptist University of Jackson. He followed farming and clerking one year and continued in the former until 1882, and from that time until January, 1886, was deputy clerk and master of the chancery court, and at the latter date became clerk and master. Mr. Hurt is a Democrat of the younger and more progressive school. He is a member of the I. O. O. F., and the Methodist Episcopal Church South. His maternal grandfather, Matthias DeBerry, won great notoriety as sheriff in breaking up gambling institutions at an early day, also lawlessness and robbery. He was sheriff at the time the noted John A. Murrell was captured.

Henry Clay Irby, A. M., professor of mathematics in the Southwestern Baptist University at Jackson, Tenn., was born in Fayette County, Tenn., June 16, 1835. He was educated in Union University at Murfreesboro, Tenn., and graduated with the degree of A. M., in 1860. At the breaking out of the war he organized Company D, Ninth Regiment Tennessee Infantry, and served as lieutenant of the company until May, 1862, when he was elected captain. He was severely wounded at Perryville, Ky. In 1867 he founded McKenzie College (now McTyeire Institute), and was president of the same for some time. In January, 1875, he came to Jackson and accepted his present position, which he is filling in a highly satisfactory manner. November 8, 1862, he was united in marriage to Elizabeth F. Eubank, of Glasgow, Ky. The Professor is a Democrat in his political views, and is a Mason, Knights Templar degree. He is secretary of the Tennessee Baptist State Convention, and has been clerk for several years of the Central Baptist Association. He has been a member of the church since 1852.

Jos. J. Johnson, farmer, was born January 25, 1826, in Madison County, and is an only child of James and Mary Ann (O'Guinn) Johnson. The father was born in Moore County, N. C., and the mother in Fayetteville, N. C., where they were married and soon after moved to this county, locating near Cotton Grove, December, 1825, where the father worked at the tailor's trade until his death March, 1826. The mother afterward married Jos. Fry, to whom one child, Margaret Ann, now Mrs. C. H. O'Neal, of Chester County, was born. The mother outlived this husband and died in 1874. Our subject, from the time of his father's death, resided with his paternal grandparents till he reached his majority, and then farmed a place given him by his grandfather about five years; then sold this place and bought another in McNairy County, where he remained till 1863. He then joined Forrest's cavalry command and served under him until the close of the war; after which he removed to his present residence, containing seventy acres, adjoining Pinson, and embarked in the mercantile trade, which he followed about ten years, then returned to agricultural pursuits. In 1857 he married Celia Rogers, to whom one son and one daughter were born; the daughter is still living. The mother of these children died November 3, 1860, and March, 1863, he married Mary McCallum, to whom five sons and one daughter were born, all still living except one son. The mother of these children died December, 1872, and in January, 1875, he married Martha A. Lacy, to whom the following children have been born, all still living: Margaret Louisa, Salley May, Thos. Lacy. He is a member of the F. & A. M., and is identified with the Democratic party.

Amos W. Jones, A. M., D. D., president of the Memphis Conference Female Institute, is the ninth of a family of six sons and six daughters born to Amos and Mary (Myrick) Jones. He was born December 28, 1815, in Franklin County, N. C., this being the native county also of both the parents, where they were married, lived, farmed, and died, their deaths occurring at the birthplace (and where the father lived during his whole life) the mother when our subject was young, and the father in 1848. The father was a natural mechanic, but devoted most of his attention to agricultural pursuits. He was also local minister in the Methodist Church many years. Our subject entered Randolph-Macon College, Virginia, at the age of sixteen, graduating in 1839. He then spent four years as traveling minister, and accepted a professorship in the institute, of which he became president in 1853, which position he has since occupied. In 1841 he married Caroline Blanch, to which union one child was born, Amos B., president of Huntsville Female College. The mother of this child died December 10, 1841. In 1843 he married Mary E. Wamack, to which union seven children were born, the survivors being Dr. James T. Jones, of Jackson, and Mrs. Mary Anna Dashiell, of Terrell, Tex. The mother of these children died in 1853, and in 1857 Mr. Jones married Amanda C. Bigelow, five children being born, George C. and Ammatilla surviving, the former being professor and secretary of the institute faculty and the latter a student. By this marriage was born Miss Ida V., who was for several years one of the prominent instructors of the institute, and whose death occurred while visiting at Chautauqua, N. Y., August 16, 1884. The mother of these children died June 5, 1886. He fills the appointment at the institute for the Memphis Conference, to which he was admitted in 1845. George C., referred to above, was born at Jackson, Tenn., on the 29th of August, 1859, and graduated at the Southwestern Baptist University in 1876, taking the degree of A. B. He then entered Vanderbilt, taking the degree of A. M. in 1879, and was alumni orator, at the same place, in 1880, in which year he began teaching in the institute, of which he is at present the principal instructor. During school vacation, in 1882, he graduated at Comer's Commercial College, Boston, and in 1883–84 attended the department of physics and mathematics in the University of Berlin. January 14, 1885, he married Lelia L. Moore, of Terrell, Tex., to whom was born one child—Ida B., still living. The Doctor, Amos W., with his whole family, are members of the Methodist Church. He is also a member of the F. & A. M., having filled most of the prominent offices of the order. George C. is a member of the K. of P. and K. of H.

Alexander M. Jones was born in Mecklenburg County, N. C., September 18, 1823, and is the son of Julius A. Jones, who was also a North Carolinian, and immigrated to Tennessee in 1826. Before leaving his native State he was married to Martha Walker, daughter of Matthew Walker, farmer, and the fruits of their union were four sons and one daughter, our subject being the second of the family. On coming to Tennessee the family settled at Poplar Creek, and here Julius Jones followed farming until his death, August 28, 1831. His wife died August 7, 1877. Alexander M. was reared on a farm, and received such education as the limited facilities of the country afforded at that early day. January 26, 1848, he married Martha E. Montgomery, who was born March 7, 1825, and died April 17, 1859, leaving her husband and one son, Julius C., who was born May 31, 1849, to mourn her loss. January 3, 1860, Mr. Jones married Sarah J. Snodgrass, to whom one son and three daughters were born—Ada L., Rush A., Fannie B. and Martha E. Mrs. Jones was born at Snodgrass Springs, Tenn., January 1, 1829. Mr. Jones served in Col. Wilson's regiment of cavalry for some time during the war, and was in a number of hard-fought battles. After the battle of Fort Pillow, sickness prevented further service. He is a Democrat and Mason, and owns 400 acres of land about five miles from Jackson. He and Mrs. Jones are members of the Methodist Episcopal Church South.

Thomas S. Jones, proprietor of the Union Saloon and Restaurant, was born in this State in 1842, and is the son of Shelton and Mary (McLemore) Jones. The parents are also natives of this State. The father was a boot and shoe and harness-maker. He died in Lincoln County in 1844. His wife then married Patrick O'Neal. She died in 1873. Our subject was reared on a farm, and lived in different counties until 1875, when he came to this county, and after farming two years, moved to this city and engaged in the dray business, running five drays. He was in the general freight transfer business, and also dealt in coal, continuing until 1880, when he opened a family grocery and saloon in the southwestern portion of the city, and did business there for fourteen months. He sold out and went to Nashville, where he ran a saloon about twelve months, and returned to this city and again entered the saloon business here, and continued up to the present time, having recently added a restaurant. During the exposition in New Orleans, in 1883, he spent some months in that city tending bar in a very popular house. In 1861 he enlisted in the Confederate service under Col. Wm. B. Bate, ex-governor, and remained twelve months, then re-enlisted, but while home on a furlough was taken prisoner, required to take the oath and remained at home. In 1865 he was united in marriage to Miss M. E. Matthews, of Davidson County, and daughter of Buck Matthews. She was. born in this State in 1844, and is the mother of one child named Mary, who died in infancy. He and wife are both members of the church. In politics he is a Democrat.

Col. D. H. King, a prominent business man and citizen of Jackson, Tenn., is a native of Williamson County, Tenn., born February 14, 1835, son of George P. and Lucinda T. (Gooch) King, both natives of Tennessee. Subject was reared and educated in his native county; left there in 1849; followed farming three years in Carroll; came to Madison County in 1852. In 1855 came to Jackson; followed clerking one year; engaged in the retail liquor business in 1856, and continued successfully until the war. He enlisted in Forrest's cavalry in 1864, and served until the close of the war; was previous to this, however, in the quartermaster's department, being at the battle of Shiloh and other engagements of note. After the war Mr. King resumed the liquor business, in which he has been interested ever since, conducting at present a strictly first-class house in all its appointments (one of the finest in the State). He has also conducted a paying feed and commission business since 1883, and has as fine a stud of horses in his stables as can be found in West Tennessee. Col. King has taken an active interest in all public and private enterprises in the city and county. He owns a large flouring-mill and cotton-gin at Spring Creek and two good plantations in the county. On the 8th of September, 1858, he was married to Miss Sarah C. Wilson, of this county; by her he has three children, two now living: John D. (partner in the liquor business with the Colonel) and Charles H. The Colonel is an unswerving Democrat in politics, representing this county in the Legislature in 1869–71; was mayor of Jackson in 1872–76, and for many years a member of the city council. He is a member of the Encampment of I. O. O. F. He was a member of the Madison County Agricultural and Mechanical Association fourteen years, and is justly regarded as one among the enterprising and eminently successful business men and citizens of Jackson. He built King's Opera House in 1874 at an expense of $44,000, one of the finest in the South, and conducted it successfully until it burned down, March, 1883, at a loss of $22,000.

J. H. Lanier, M. D., was born in this State in 1840, and is the son of J. H. and Cassandra (Barham) Lanier. The parents came to Tennessee, when quite young, from Virginia and North Carolina respectively. The father was a life-long farmer, living on the farm on which our subject now resides for fifty years, having died here in 1882, his widow following him in death in 1885. The grandfather of our subject commanded a company in the war of 1812, his name being J. M. Lanier. The Lanier family are descendants of the Huguenots, two brothers having been expelled from France in 1685, on account of their religion, and came to Virginia and settled in the town of Maniken, and from them sprang the Lanier family in the United States. Our subject was reared on a farm, and is living on a portion of the farm of his birth. He received his literary education at the Southwestern Baptist University in Jackson, Tenn. In 1860 he began reading medicine, and attended the sessions of 1860–61 of the Jefferson Medical College at Philadelphia; and in May, 1861, he enlisted as a private in the Confederate service, and remained until May, 1865. He received a flesh wound in the arm while engaged in the battle at Franklin. After returning from the army he resumed the study of medicine, attending the University of Nashville in 1865–66, graduating in the latter year. He has since been engaged in the practice of medicine, conducting his farm at the same time. December 20, 1866, he married Miss Mary E. Christian, of Carroll County, and daughter of A. B. and Eliza O. Christian. She was born in this State in 1848, and is the mother of ten children—three daughters and seven sons. The wife died October 20, 1885. He and wife were members of the Methodist Episcopal Church. He is a member of the Masonic order, and politically a Democrat. He was married the second time to Miss E. J. Moffitt, of Lexington, Tenn., December 8, 1886. Miss Moffitt is the daughter of J. M. and Harriet Moffitt, of Henderson.

Andrew B. Langford, of the firm of Conger & Langford, millers, was born in North Carolina in 1832, and came to Tennessee with his father when three years of age. He is the son of William and Judah (Peel) Langford. They are natives of North Carolina. The father was a farmer by occupation, and was moderately prosperous in life. They were the parents of nine children. The mother died in 1834. The father married for his second wife, Sarah Futrell; she died about 1859. The father died in 1878. Our subject was reared to manhood on the farm, and then engaged in the saddlery business in this city for four years. He then conducted a photograph gallery in this city for about twenty-six years, after which he engaged in his present business, which has proven very successful. Mr. Langford began life poor, having gained his possession by his own honesty, energy and perseverance. In 1860 he was united in marriage to Miss Rebecca Carter, of this county. She was born in 1843, and became the mother of one child, who lived but one month. In 1866 he married for his second wife, Mrs. Cora C. Conger, who was born in 1844, and is the mother of seven children, three of whom are dead. His wife died in 1883. He has taken all the degrees in Masonry, including the Knights Templar degree. He is a member of the I. O. O. F., including the encampment, and K. of H. In politics he is Democratic.

John R. Lewis was born in Williamson County, Tenn., February 2, 1838. His father, Richard F. Lewis, was a native of Virginia, born near Prince Edward Court House, and came to Tennessee with his parents when but seven years of age, locating in Rutherford County. Here he was reared and educated, and on attaining his majority went to Williamson County, where he married Ann M. Roberts, daughter of Ben. Roberts, a farmer and native of Virginia. The family, of which our subject was the second member, consisted of five sons and three daughters; five are now living. The father was a farmer, and was married in 1853, and died in Madison County July 7, 1863. His wife was born in Williamson County, and died June 28, 1884. John R. Lewis received a limited education, and has made farming his chief calling through life. He enlisted in the Sixth Tennessee Infantry, under Col. W. H. Stevens, and was a participant in the battles of Chickamauga, Harrisburg, Knoxville, Brice's Cross-roads, and numerous battles and skirmishes of less note. In the early part of the war he was discharged from the infantry service for disability, but on recovering, joined the cavalry and served under Gen. Forrest. At the battle of Chickamauga he was cut off with Longstreet's corps and covered his retreat from Knoxville. He was captured and taken to Nashville, but was soon paroled through the influence of Provisional Gov. Andrew Johnson. He served through the entire war, and three weeks before the general surrender returned home on sick furlough. He was married in Madison County, February 7, 1860, to Jane Baker, a daughter of Henry Baker, and by her became the father of the following children: Richard H., John (deceased), and Samuel C. Mrs. Lewis was born in Madison County, December 27, 1841. Mr. Lewis is a Democrat, and belongs to the Masonic, K. of H. and A. O. U. W. fraternities. He and wife are members of the Missionary Baptist Church, and he is a farmer and owns 137 acres of land.

Edmund Skinner Mallory, attorney at law, was born in Hampton, Va., September 22, 1846. He is the son of Charles K. and Martha (Skinner) Mallory, who were born in Virginia and North Carolina, respectively. Our subject's ancestors settled in their respective States in early colonial days; his grandfather, Charles K. Mallory, having been lieutenant-governor of Virginia during the war of 1812. His great-grandfather, Col. Francis Mallory, was killed at Bethel in the Revolutionary war. Edmund S. Mallory was reared in his native State, and graduated from the law department of the University of Virginia, June

29, 1866. In the beginning of 1864 he entered in the Virginia Military Institute, and served under Breckinridge in the Valley campaign of that year, and remained in the service around Richmond and Petersburg until the final surrender. He began practicing law in Hampton, and in 1869 came to Jackson, Tenn., and is now one of the first lawyers of the county. He is an unswerving and active Democrat in politics, and was a prominent candidate for attorney-general and reporter of Tennessee in 1886, but did not secure the election. September 18, 1872, he married Jennie, daughter of J. M. Parker, of Jackson, and three living children are the fruits of their union: John P., Charles K. and Callie P. Mr. Mallory and family are members of the Episcopal Church, and he is a K. of P. and Past Grand Chancellor of the State. He was a delegate to the general convention of his church at Chicago in 1886, and is considered one of the first citizens of the county.

William C. Marshall, a citizen of Pinson, was born May, 1837, in McNairy County, and is one of a family consisting of nine children born to William W. and Sarah C. (Holloway) Marshall, of which our subject, one brother and four sisters are the surviving members. The father was a native of Tennessee, and the mother of Virginia. They were married in Williamson County, this State, where they farmed until about 1828, then came to Madison County and remained five years; then moved to McNairy County, residing there about the same length of time, after which they returned to this county, locating near Pinson, where they farmed until their deaths, the mother dying in 1863, and the father in 1884. At the commencement of the war, William C. enlisted in the Sixth Tennessee Confederate Infantry, as private, but soon received promotion in the following order, viz.: Fourth sergeant, orderly sergeant, third lieutenant and first lieutenant, discharging the duties of the last named office from the battle of Perryville until the close of the war. He participated in the battles of Shiloh, Perryville, Chickamauga, Missionary Ridge, the Georgia campaign, etc. After the war he taught school a few terms in Madison County; then ran a saw-mill in Pinson one year, since which time he has filled clerkships in different mercantile firms of Pinson, at present being connected with the store of M. M. Robins. He has a residence and several acres of land in Pinson, and is considered one of the prominent, substantial citizens of the village. In 1870 he married Margaret E. Anderson, and to them have been born the following children: Emma, Mellie, Robert A., Hulon E., Maggie, and one dying in infancy. He and family are members of the Methodist Church. He is a Democrat in politics.

Rufus M. Mason is a native of the Empire State, his birth occurring in 1818. His father, George Mason, was born in the old Bay State, and about 1816 moved to New York State. His occupation through life was farming, and he was a member of the Free-Will Baptist Church, and a man of more than ordinary force of character. His first wife was Lydia Hathaway, of Massachusetts, who bore him ten children and died in 1839. She was a worthy woman, and was born in 1792. His second wife was Wealthy Cole, of Ohio. The father was born in 1790, and died in May, 1865. Rufus M. was reared to the vocation of farming, and when twenty-one years of age began traveling, locating finally in Ohio, where he attended school the better part of three years. He then came to Tennessee and located at Spring Creek, Madison County, and taught school until 1847, when he began merchandising in partnership with J. F. Clark. In 1851 he and his brother-in-law purchased a farm, upon which he located. The most of the time from 1855 to 1858 he taught school; then remained on the farm until 1861, and then enlisted to help erect Fort Pillow. He was finally appointed to the secret service by Gen. Beauregard, but returned home in 1862, and took no further part in the war. October 8, 1850, he married Eunice A. Doak, of this county, daughter of Capt. William and Jane (Wilson) Doak, the father having been an officer in the war of 1812. This lady was born in 1830, and is the mother of three sons and six daughters; one daughter died in infancy, and three other daughters died after becoming grown. The mother died in 1880. She was a Methodist, as is her husband. He has taken all the degrees of Masonry, including the commandery degree. From 1865 to 1871 he merchandised at Spring Creek, but has since conducted his farm. He has served as justice of the peace about twelve years. He affiliates with the Democratic party.

Edward Samuel Matthews is a Madison County Tennessean, born on the 14th of January, 1832. His father, Maj. Edward W. Matthews, was born in Virginia, March 27, 1802, and immigrated to Tennessee with his parents when a small boy. He settled near Nolensville, Williamson County, and there married Mary R. Ralston, daughter of Alexander Ralston, who was a soldier in the war of 1812, and a participant in the battle of New Orleans. To Mr. and Mrs. Matthews six children were born. The father is a gentleman of the old school, with a vast fund of information and a very agreeable conversationalist. He is residing with our subject, and is eighty-five years of age. His wife was born in Middle Tennessee, August 26, 1805, and died at her home, October 15, 1886. At the time of her death she and her husband had been married sixty-two years. Their descendants numbered sixty-five, including children, grandchildren and great-grandchildren. Edward S. Matthews, our subject, attended the common schools, and was married in Madison County April 14,1859, to Martha A. Smith. [Her parents' history is given in a sketch of John M. Smith.] They became the parents of ten children, nine now living: Sallie R., Edward W., Lucy E., Mary S., Maggie L., James S., Mattie F., Alex. R. and Nettie R. The mother of these children was born in Rutherford County October 29, 1839. Mr. Matthews is a Democrat, and he and wife and two daughters are members of the church. He owns 660 acres of land.

Judge Henry W. McCorry, attorney at law, of Jackson, Tenn., and native of Madison County, was born March 25, 1845; son of Henry W. and Corinna A. (Henderson) McCorry, natives respectively of Tennessee and North Carolina. Henry W. McCorry, Sr., was brought to West Tennessee about 1828 or 1829 by his father, Thomas McCorry, who was a large land owner in East and West Tennessee. He was one of the sterling pioneer citizens of the county, and was of Irish descent. Judge McCorry's maternal grandfather was the celebrated Col. Tom Henderson, of North Carolina. Our subject secured a good literary education in Madison County. He enlisted as a private in Company G, Col. Biffles' Ninth Tennessee Cavalry, and served from June, 1863, until 1865. After his return home he entered the Lebanon (Tenn.), Law School and graduated from the same in 1867. He began practicing in Jackson in 1867, and with S. Caruthers, Esq., continued until 1871. He and Gen. Campbell were then partners until 1874. In 1875 he was appointed judge of the common law and chancery court of Madison County, and filled this important office very satisfactorily until 1882, when he resigned to resume the practice of his profession, and has since been associated with C. G. Bond, Esq., in a large and lucrative practice. In 1885 he was appointed by President Cleveland, United States Attorney for West Tennessee, and is now holding that position. In December, 1868, he married Miss Lucy P. Cole, of Brownsville, Tenn. They have three sons and five daughters who are living. The Judge is a Democrat and has taken an active interest in local and national politics. He was a delegate to the convention at Chicago that nominated President Cleveland, and belongs to the K. of P. and I. O. O. F. fraternities. He is a judge and lawyer of experience and ability, and is one of the first citizens of Jackson.

Samuel D. McDonald, a prominent farmer, was born in Madison County, Tenn., November 10, 1835. His father, James B. McDonald, was born in Halifax County, Va., and was brought to Tennessee by his parents when an infant. He was married three times, the first time to Miss Vaughn; the second time to Annie Duty, which union resulted in the birth of four children; and the third time to Charity E. Langford, of Madison County, to whom were born three sons and two daughters, our subject being the fourth member of the family. The father served as sheriff of Madison County for a period of four years, and died in Carroll County, Tenn., in 1866. His wife was born in North Carolina, and died also in Carroll County in 1868. Samuel D. McDonald received the advantages of the common schools and has followed the life of a farmer. He served in the Twenty-second Tennessee Regiment, under Col. Thomas J. Freeman, afterward consolidated with the Twelfth Tennessee Infantry, under Col. Bell of Dyer County. Mr. McDonald was at Belmont, Murfreesboro, Chickamauga, Missionary Ridge and was in the famous retreat and almost continuous fight from Dalton to Atlanta. He was wounded twice in the same day in front of Atlanta, at Peach Tree Creek. After this he returned to his home on furlough, but being cut off from his command, was prevented from further duty during the remainder of the war. He was married in the house in which he now lives, November 4, 1869, to Mrs. E. C. McDonald, daughter of Philip Warlick, and to their union were born two children—Samuel and Carrie Emma. Mrs. McDonald was born May 30, 1838. The family lived at Louisville, Ky., from 1870 to 1880, during which time the two children named above were born. Mrs. McDonald's parents, Mr. and Mrs. Warlick, were born in North Carolina and Virginia, and died in 1844 and 1877 respectively. Mr. McDonald is a Democrat and owns 500 acres of good land. He and wife are members of the old school Presbyterian Church.

Capt. James T. McCutchen, cotton broker of Jackson, Tenn., was born in Carroll County, April 15, 1833; son of Col. William and Matilda (Collins) McCutchen, who were born in Virginia and Maryland respectively. James T. came to Madison County in 1847, and learned the printer's trade, at which he worked throughout the States until the war. He was in California at the time, but returned home and organized a company of Western men and served as captain of Company A, Fourth Regiment, Arizona Confederate troops, under Price and Kirby Smith. After his return home he revived the West Tennessee *Whig*, and with W. W. Gates conducted it one year. He then engaged in his present cotton business and has met with good success financially. In 1886 he accepted the position as editor of the *Tribune and Sun*, of Jackson. In 1867 he married Miss Annie T. Adamson, of Madison County, and they have four sons and five daughters living. The Captain is a Democrat in politics and has served a number of years as chairman of the Madison County Democratic Executive Committee. He is a member of the K. of H., and is one of the eminent business men of Jackson. He is the oldest cotton buyer outside of Memphis, in West Tennessee. His father was a soldier in the war of 1812, and afterward wrote some very interesting articles about the same, which have been handed down to posterity as history.

Rev. Edward B. McNeil was born in Franklin County, Tenn., August 13, 1837; son of Alfred D. and Ruth (Corn) McNeil, natives, respectively, of Tennessee and Virginia. Edward B. McNeil was taken by his parents to Mississippi, when he was about twelve years of age and there resided until twenty years of age. He then entered Union University at Murfreesboro, Tenn., but was obliged to give up school life, owing to the breaking out of the war. He enlisted in the Confederate Army and served three years and nine months in the Forty-first Regiment Mississippi Infantry. In April, 1866, he was ordained a regular minister in the Baptist Church and followed his chosen calling for twelve years at Booneville, Miss. In 1881 he came to Jackson, Tenn., where he has since resided, being in charge of several churches in West Tennessee. October 13, 1867, he married Miss Jessie A. Kittredge, who was born in Louisiana. She died December 7, 1883, having borne six sons. Mr. McNeil has been local editor of the Jackson *Dispatch* for the past year. He is a Democrat, a Mason and a member of the K. of H.

F. H. Mayo, a prominent merchant of this city, was born in this county in 1846, and is the son of C. 'B. and Caroline Mayo. The father is a farmer by occupation. The mother died in 1866, and in 1884 the father married Mrs. Clay Kendrick. Our subject was reared to the age of seventeen on the farm, then enlisted in the Confederate service, Company C, Thirteenth Tennessee Regiment, in Gen. N. B. Forrest's cavalry, and remained two years, being the close of the war. In 1867 he came to this city, and after spending some months clerking, engaged in the mercantile business, which he continues up to the present time, and has become very popular, having recently agreed to furnish the members of the Agricultural Wheel all their goods at reduced prices. In politics he is a stanch Democrat.

Marcus H. Meeks is a native of McNairy County, Tenn., and was born May 9, 1852, being the son of John H. and Eleanor (Atkins) Meeks, natives respectively of Tennessee and North Carolina. The father is now a prominent citizen and farmer of McNairy County. Marcus H. was reared on his father's farm, securing a good education in youth, taking a special course in the University of Tennessee, at Knoxville. In 1876 he entered the Lebanon Law School, and in 1877 graduated therefrom, and then began to practice in his native county. In August, 1878, he was elected attorney-general of the Eleventh Judicial Circuit, and served one term of eight years. In August, 1886, he came to Jackson, and began practicing with the firm of Pitts & Hays, under the firm name of Pitts, Hays & Meeks, and has continued thus until the present. December 1, 1880, he was united in marriage with Miss Annie Baldwin Nunnelly, of Hickman County. They have two children—Emmett A. and Loraine. Mr. Meeks is a Democrat, and he and wife are members of the Christian Church.

Keith S. Moffat, a prominent grocer of this city, was born in Florida in 1854, and is the son of Alexander and Margie A. (Singletary) Moffat. The father was born in Scotland and came to Florida, where he married. He was a carpenter by trade and had a family of four children. The father died in 1865. The mother lives in this city. Our subject was reared to manhood in Florida, having come to this place in 1878. After coming to the city he was employed on the Mobile & Ohio Railroad, which engagement continued until December, 1885, when he opened a family grocery in East Jackson, and in October, 1886, moved to his present location on Market Street, where he is receiving a fair share of deserved patronage. Mr. Moffat began life poor, his possessions being gained by his own honesty and fair dealing. December 6, 1882, he married Laura Estes, of this city. She was born in this county in 1867, and is the mother of three children: Alexander, Nellie and Edward A. He and wife are members of the Baptist Church. He is a member of the Locomotive Brotherhood and in politics is a Democrat.

P. J. Murray, secretary Jackson Oil-Mills, was born August, 1846, in Cook County, Ill., and is of a family of seven children born to P. J. and Anna Murray, both natives of Ireland. The parents both came to America when young and married in Chicago, where the mother's death occurred in 1857. The father is still living in Chicago, having retired from the mercantile trade about 1865. Our subject and three brothers are the surviving members of the family. He remained with his parents till the commencement of the war; then was appointed to the United States military telegraph service, and at the close of the war continued telegraphy at Memphis, Tenn., till 1878; then came to Jackson and accepted a position as cashier of the oil-mills established here at that time, with a stock capital of $40,000. At the incorporation of the company the following officers were elected: President, John H. Freeman; vice-president, John L. Wisdom; J. W. Allison, secretary; N. H. White, treasurer, and our subject, cashier. The officers were unchanged till September, 1886, except by death of Freeman, Howel E. Jackson acting president, at which date J. W. Allison was elected president; P. J. Murray, secretary, White and Wisdom retaining their old offices. In 1883 the amount of capital was increased to $100,000. The company transacts a business of about $300,000 annually. In 1873 our subject married Eloisa McPherson, of Missouri, to whom five sons and one daughter have been born, all still living: Henry M., Anna, Cornie, P. James, Ernest and Victor. He and family are members of the Episcopal Church. He is also a member of the F. & A. M., I. O. O. F., K. T., K. P., K. of H. and K. & L. of H. Politically, he is a Democrat.

M. Murchison, M. D., was born in North Carolina in 1823, and came to this State with his parents in 1839. His father, William Murchison, was a native of North Carolina, and was a successful farmer by occupation. His mother, Isabella (Reid) Murchison, was also a native of North Carolina, and bore her husband ten children—five sons and five daughters—only four of which family are now living. The father was a man of more than ordinary mental force, and served in the North Carolina Senate for about twenty years, acquiring a State reputation for legislative work. His death occurred about 1849, and that of his wife in 1855. Both were members of the Presbyterian Church, of which he was an elder for many years. Our subject was reared on a farm, and was educated at the subscription schools. He spent a few years in trading in stock, and in 1849 began the study of medicine and attended the Philadelphia College of Medicine in 1850-51, graduating in the latter year. In May, 1851, he married Frances A. Alston, the adopted daughter of John R. Alston, who was born in 1832, and has presented her husband with five children, the two now living being William and Duncan. After his graduation in medicine he located for practice in Denmark, and here he has since remained. In 1862 he enlisted in the Confederate service, and was made captain of Company D, of the Fifty-second Tennessee Regiment. When the army left Corinth he returned home. He is a Democrat, an Odd Fellow, and he and wife are members of the Presbyterian Church. He owns a farm of 100 acres five miles east of Denmark.

Hon. David L. Murrell, dry goods merchant of Jackson, Tenn., native of Madison County, born May 9, 1856, is a son of Thomas and Eliza (Beattie) Murrell, both natives of Ireland. David L. was reared and educated in this county. He first engaged in the dry goods business as clerk with his father, who came to Jackson in 1845 and engaged in the mercantile business with his brother—Lindsay Murrell. In 1884 our subject succeeded this firm in business, carrying a full and select stock of dry goods and shoes, controlling a fair share of the trade in this line in the city and county. August 21, 1878, he married Miss Leila S. Morgan, of Memphis, a native of Murfreesboro, Tenn. They have two sons—David

L. and Marian M. Mr. Murrell is a Democrat in politics and was a "floterial" representative for Madison and Henderson Counties in the State Legislature in 1884–85. He is a member of the K. of H. Himself and wife are members of the First Presbyterian Church, of this city, and he is recognized as one among the reliable and enterprising business men of Jackson.

Judge Thomas C. Muse is a native of Pittsylvania County, Va., and was born January 23, 1834, being the son of Daniel C. and Eliza (Stone) Muse, both of whom were natives of the Old Dominion. These parents came to Tennessee when Thomas C. was an infant two or three years old, and located in Henderson County, where the father died in 1865. Thomas C. was reared on a farm, securing in youth a fair schooling, and later attending an academy at Clinton, Ky., where he completed his literary education. In 1854 he entered the law department of Cumberland University and the following year graduated, and the same year began practicing at Lexington, Tenn., continuing this until the breaking out of the war. In 1865 he came to Jackson and continued to practice, but during that year served in the State Senate with distinction, to which position he had been elected before coming to Jackson. After two years of practice he was appointed chancellor of this division, and was elected to this high office in 1868, serving until 1870, when he was removed by the provisions of the new constitution. Upon the vacation of the office of judge of the common law and chancery court of the county of Madison by Judge McCorry, Judge Muse was appointed by Gov. Hawkins to the position, and at the next general election he was elected to fill out the unexpired term of Judge McCorry, which he did in a highly efficient manner, the term expiring September, 1886. Judge Muse was formerly an old line Whig, and during the war was a firm supporter of the Union cause. Since the formation of the Republican party, he has been one of its most zealous and effective followers in this portion of the State. He has two living sons by his first wife, Elizabeth C. (Collier) Muse, who died in 1871. In 1872 he married his present wife—Mrs. Theresa Smedley. Mr. Muse is a K. T. in Masonry, and is one of the most prominent citizens in this portion of the State.

William T. Nelson, vice-president of the Second National Bank of Jackson, Tenn., was born in Rutherford County, Tenn., February 21, 1848; son of William D. and Martha (Henderson) Nelson, who were born in the Blue-grass State. William T. removed to Shelby County, Tenn., with his parents when about twelve years of age, and secured an excellent education at La Grange (Tenn.) College and Louisville (Ky.)

High School.   On his father's side of the family he is a descendant of
Col. Nelson, of Revolutionary fame, and on his mother's side he is the
grandson of Isham Henderson, who was a relative of Thomas Jefferson,
and studied law under him.   Isham was offered his choice of positions
in Jefferson's cabinet, but refused, and was afterward nominated governor of Kentucky, which position he also refused.   William D. Nelson,
father of our subject, was a successful business man and an elder in the
Presbyterian Church.   William T. has followed agricultural pursuits
principally since the war, and owns at the present time a number of plantations in this and Shelby counties and also in Arkansas.   In 1882 he
removed to Jackson, and in September, 1886, accepted the position of
vice-president in the Second National Bank, being one of the organizers
and stockholders of same.   He and Rebecca Hurt were united in
marriage in 1875, and two sons and three daughters have been born to
their union.   One son was born to Mr. Nelson's former marriage with
Mattie De Berry (deceased).   Mr. Nelson votes the Democratic ticket
and is an elder in the Kerrville (Shelby County) Presbyterian Church.
He is considered one of the first citizens of Jackson.

Samuel J. Nowell was born in Madison County, April 19, 1841.
His father, Dempsy Nowell, was a native of North Carolina, and came to
this county when a young man.   He here married Harriet Piercy, who
bore him eight sons, seven of whom grew to manhood, our subject being
the sixth of this family.   The father was a prosperous farmer through
life, and died near Denmark about the year 1850.   The mother was born
in North Carolina, and at the age of thirteen years came with her parents to Tennessee.   She is now living with her son, James H., in this
county.   Samuel J. grew up on the farm, with a limited education, and
has made farming his chief occupation.   He is a Democrat.   When the
late war broke out he opposed the secession of Tennessee.   His first
presidential vote was polled for Seymour and Blair.   He owns ninety-six
acres five miles northeast of Jackson, on the Illinois Central Railroad.   He is
comfortably situated, and has an attractive home.   July 10, 1864, he
married Mrs. Martha J. Carter, daughter of John Young.   This lady has
borne her husband two children: John Henry and Joab.   She was born
in this county October 25, 1847.   Husband and wife are members of the
Methodist Episcopal Church South.

James H. Nowell, is the son of Dempsy Nowell, and was born in
this county February 8, 1830.   The father was born in Bertie County,
N. C., in 1805, and immigrated to this county when a young man.   He
married Harriet, daughter of Cader Piercy. [See sketch of Samuel J. Nowell.]   James H. was the oldest of his father's family.   The mother was

born in Bertie County, N. C., March 26, 1810, and is yet living with her son, James H. The latter follows the vocation of farming. He received a limited education in youth. February 8, 1854, he married Miss Frankie J., daughter of Thomas Jackson. This lady was born in East Tennessee, October 24, 1854, and when four months old was brought to Madison County. Of the twelve children born to Mr. and Mrs. Nowell, eight are now living: John T., Dempsy M., Samuel A., James A., Mary M., Frances A., Nannie E. and Ida M. Mr. Nowell is a Democrat, and polled his first presidential vote for Franklin Pierce. He and wife as well as his parents are members of the Methodist Episcopal Church South. He owns 625 acres of land twelve miles north of Jackson, and has a pleasant home.

Grattan E. O'Connor, deputy clerk of the supreme court of Tennessee, at Jackson, is a native of Madison County, Tenn.; was born July 24, 1855; son of James and Annie (James) O'Connor, natives respectively, of Wexford, Ireland and Virginia. Our subject was reared and educated in this county, attending West Tennessee College, of Jackson. He spent a number of years in the mercantile business with his father in this city, and in 1879 entered the Lebanon Law School, graduated in 1880, and soon after his return, accepted the position of deputy clerk of the supreme court, which position he has filled in a faithful and efficient manner, almost continuously, up to the present time. September 1, 1885, he married in Corinth, Miss., Miss Nettie R. Russell, a native of Hardin County, Tenn. They have one daughter—Kathleen. Mr. O'Connor is a Democrat in political views, being of the younger and more progressive school of Democracy. He is a member of the K. P., and justly recognized as one among the enterprising and successful younger citizens of Jackson, and a popular public official.

Samuel M. Ozier was born in Madison County, Tenn., on the 16th of June, 1844. His father, William Ozier, was a native of North Carolina, born May 28, 1804, and an early immigrant to Tennessee. He soon after married Mary Smith, and moved to Carroll County, where he resided eight years. He then became a resident of Madison County. He also resided for some time in McNairy County. He became the father of eight children; one of his sons, Green G. Ozier, was killed at Atlanta during the late war. The father was a farmer, and died in Henderson, August 16, 1879. His wife was born December 14, 1810, and is yet living at the old homestead. Samuel M. was reared on a farm two and a half miles from his present home. He received a fair English education, and has made farming his chief business through life. He served in the Confederate Army as first lieutenant of Company I, Russell's regiment, Bell's brigade and Forrest's command, and was in many hotly contested battles. He served with Hood throughout his entire Tennessee campaign, and was surrendered at Gainesville, Ala., May 11, 1865. September 26, 1866, he married Annie Cook, daughter of A. P. Cook, a merchant and manufacturer. To Mr. and Mrs. Ozier, five children have been born, three of whom are living: Maud L., Roy L. and Terry Samuel. Mrs. Ozier was born in Maury County, Tenn., August 19, 1839. Mr. Ozier is a Democrat, and cast his first presidential vote for Horace Greeley. He owns 700 acres of excellent land, and he and wife and two daughters are members of the Methodist Episcopal Church South.

J. J. Pardue, merchant at Claybrook, was born in this State in 1833; is the son of Isaac H. and Sarah (Davis) Pardue. The parents are natives of North Carolina and Tennessee, respectively, the father coming to Tennessee about 1815. He was a life-long farmer, being moderately prosperous, and supported a family of twelve children, four daughters and eight sons; five of the children are yet living. The father moved to Mississippi in 1847, where he lived until his death, which occurred in 1870, being sixty-eight years of age. Our subject was reared on a farm, and was a first-class farmer. He went to Mississippi with his father in 1847, and remained until 1861, when he returned to Tennessee and enlisted in the Confederate service, Sixth Tennessee Regiment, and remained until after Hood's raid to Nashville, and then returned home. May 7, 1861, he married Mrs. Catherine (Brown) Moore, widow of Nathan Moore, by whom she had three children: Ellen, Mary and Lucy. She was born in this State in 1829, and is the mother of two children by her last marriage, namely: Rosa L. and Laura. Rosa L. died in 1881, being eighteen years old. At the close of the war, our subject remained in Tennessee, and resumed farming, continuing until 1879, when he began merchandising in this village, and commands a large and remuenrative trade. He has two good farms—one of 112 acres, and one of 172 acres—and owns the property in which he does business and in which he lives in this village. He and family are members of the Methodist Episcopal Church South. In politics he is strictly Democratic.

David H. Parker, M. D., was born in North Carolina, in 1832, and is the son of Henry S. and Susan F. (Pinkston) Parker, both of whom were natives of North Carolina and came to Tennessee in 1832. The father was a successful farmer and raised a family of eight children of nine born to himself and wife. He was a useful citizen, his death occurring in this county, April 15, 1855, his wife following him to the grave, March 10, 1870. David H. was reared as a farmer, passing his youth without note-

worthy event, and in 1850 beginning the study of medicine, continuing a
year and a half.   In the autumn of 1851 he entered the Botanical Medical College at Memphis, from which institution he graduated in 1853.
He returned to the village where he now lives, and commenced the practice which he has continued until the present time.   In 1853 he married
Maria T. D. Reeves, of this county, daughter of Mauldin and Nancy
Reeves, who was born in this State in 1826, and is the mother of three
children, two of whom are yet living: Sarah E. (wife of Dr. Geo. Lacy)
and Susan F. (wife of William T. Pope).   Dr. and Mrs. Parker are members of the Methodist Episcopal Church South.   He is a Mason and a
Democrat, and in 1886 was elected justice of the peace.

Hon. Jonathan D. Pearson is a North Carolinian, born January 10,
1831.   His father, William Pearson, was born in the same State June 1,
1810, and in 1828 married Miss Eliza Williams, daughter of Dudley
Williams, a farmer and native of North Carolina.   Their union resulted
in the birth of three sons and two daughters, our subject being the eldest
of the family.   In 1865 William Pearson moved to Madison County,
where he followed farming, and died October 12, 1878.   The mother was
born in North Carolina, February 15, 1811, and died at the homestead,
July 27, 1873.   Jonathan D., our subject, was educated in the common
schools and from boyhood has followed the occupation of farming.   He
was married in Fayette County, Tenn., December 18, 1851, to Rebecca
C. Holland, daughter of William Holland, a native of North Carolina,
who is now living above Little Rock, Ark.   Mr. and Mrs. Pearson have
eight children: Nannie E. (Mrs. Blackmon), William M., James C.,
Mary E. (Mrs. McCallum), John L., Seban W., Walter L. and Needham
B.   Mrs. Pearson was born in Carroll County, Tenn., December 30,
1833, and died July 27, 1885.   After his marriage Mr. Pearson resided
in Henderson County until 1867, when in company with his father he moved
to his present home in Madison County.   He has been magistrate of his
district since 1872 and chairman of the county court over three years.
He is now representing Henderson and Madison Counties in the Forty-
fifth General Assembly of the State.   He is a Democrat and cast his first
presidential vote for Gen. Scott.   He is a member of the Cumberland
Presbyterian Church, and is the owner of about 700 acres of land situated about twelve miles northeast of Jackson.

John S. Pearson is a native of the old North State, and was born in
1833 to the marriage of William and Eliza (Williams) Pearson.   In
1834 his parents came to Henderson County, Tenn., and remained there
until 1865, when he came to Madison County and lived there until his
death, in 1878, his worthy wife preceding him five years. The parents were

both natives of North Carolina and were farmers, and to them were born seven children, four of whom reached years of maturity. John S. spent his youth at work on 'the farm, and has made farming his occupation through life, and has been quite successful. In 1858 he married Martha J. Olive, of Henderson County, daughter of Howell Olive. This lady was born in 1841 and has presented her husband with four sons and four daughters, one of the latter being deceased. In 1865 Mr. Pearson moved to Madison County, locating on his present farm, which lies in the eastern part of the county and consists of 400 acres of well improved land. Mr. Pearson and wife are useful citizens, kind neighbors, and are members of the Cumberland Presbyterian Church. Mr. Pearson is a stanch Democrat.

James L. Phillips, a Henderson County Tennessean, was born January 1, 1829. His father, Thomas P. Phillips, was born in Chatham County, N. C., in 1799, and immigrated to Tennessee in 1826, locating in Henderson County. He was a farmer, and served his district as magistrate for sixteen years. His death occurred September 4, 1882. His wife was born in North Carolina, and died in Henderson County in 1835. James L. was reared on a farm and was given a common school education. He has made farming his business through life, and February 8, 1848, he married Emily E. O'Neal, who was born in Henderson County in 1831, and died January 29, 1873. She was a daughter of Laban O'Neal, a farmer and native of Middle Tennessee, who moved to West Tennessee in 1830, and died in 1851. Mr. and Mrs. Phillips became the parents of the following children: Thomas L., Sarah M., Mary E., Swaine H., Lou M., Alice G., James A. and Minerva J. Of this family Sarah M., Mary E. and Swaine H. died in 1873. February 9, 1875, Mr. Phillips married Miss V. C. Hopper, daughter of Turley Hopper, a farmer, and by her became the father of two children: Rada and Lizzie. His present wife was born May 31, 1855. Mr. Phillips is a Democrat and Mason, and has represented his lodge in the Grand Lodge of the State several times. He has served as magistrate of his district since 1856, except during the war. Prior to that time he served in Henderson County, and since that time in Madison County. He has been county surveyor for the last six years, and is the owner of over 500 acres of land about eight miles from Jackson.

David T. Pope, of the firm of Pope & Blackard, liverymen, of Jackson, Tenn., was born in Madison County in 1844, son of William and Mary (Strayhorn) Pope, who were born in Virginia and North Carolina, respectively. The father was a farmer and he and wife were members of the Cumberland Presbyterian Church for many years. His wife died in 1859 and he in 1877.   David T. Pope was reared on a farm, and in the fall of 1861 enlisted in the Confederate service, in the Sixth Regiment, Tennessee Infantry.   After one year's service he joined the Seventh Tennessee Cavalry and was detached to Pemberton's escort during the siege of Vicksburg.   He was taken prisoner and paroled.   At the expiration of his parole he was exchanged and rejoined the army, serving with Hood during his memorable raid into Tennessee.   He surrendered at Gainesville, Ala., at the close of the war.   In 1866 he married Alice Newly, who was born in Tennessee in 1847.   She became the mother of four daughters and one son.   Mr. and Mrs. Pope are members of the Cumberland Presbyterian Church, and in politics Mr. Pope is a Democrat.   He has resided in Jackson since 1883, and is a prosperous liveryman of the town.

Prof. Edwin W. Price, of Jackson, Tenn., was born in Hardeman County, Tenn., January 22, 1836, son of Edwin S. and Mildred A. (Wood) Price, who were Virginians by birth.   The father came west after attaining his majority (about 1830) and located first in North Alabama and later removed to our subject's native county and State, where he died November 19, 1853.   Edwin W. attended Bethel College in Carroll County, Tenn., where he secured a good classical education, leaving that institution in July, 1855, with first honors.   After teaching school a year he then entered the Lebanon (Tenn.) Law School, from which he graduated in 1858.   He then practiced his profession in Somerville, Tenn., until the breaking out of the late war.   Early in the spring of 1861 he enlisted in Company D, Fourth Regiment Tennessee Volunteers in behalf of the Southern Confederacy, and served until the close of the war. After the surrender he commenced teaching school in Hardeman County, Tenn., and taught there until September, 1884, when he was elected to the position of professor of mathematics in the Jackson City schools, which position he holds at the present time.   January 24, 1867, he married Candace T. McGuire, of Hardeman County, and two children have blessed their union: Lizzie W. and Mary E. Price.   Prof. Price is considered an educator of experience and ability, and is a Democrat in his political views and a member of the K. of H. fraternity.

Greenville H. Ramsey, a prominent grocer of this city, was born in Tennessee in 1835, and is the son of N. P. and Polly A. (Davis) Ramsey. The parents are natives of Tennessee and Kentucky, respectively.   The mother's father was the first magistrate elected in Daviess County, Ky. The father of our subject was a prosperous farmer, and supported a family of thirteen children.   He was the first tax collector elected in Gibson County, Tenn., and his record stands above all others as a collector up to date. His home was near Trenton, where he lived until his death, which occurred in 1862; his wife following him in death about six weeks later. Our subject was reared to manhood in his native county (Gibson), and received his education in Andrew College, at Trenton. He began merchandising in early life, and with the exception of six years he spent in brick-making and contracting, continues so to the present time. In January, 1860, he moved to this city, and in the same year was united in marriage to Miss Lou Blake, of Trenton, daughter of Rev. N. O. Blake. She was born in 1840, and died in 1864, leaving one daughter, named Julia L., who married a railroad superintendent at Atlanta, Ga. In 1869 he was united in marriage to Mrs. M. L. (Ford) Arnold, widow of John Arnold, formerly a merchant of this city. She was born in this State in 1836. He and wife are members of the First Methodist Church, and he has been a steward in the church for many years. He has taken all the degrees in Masonry, including the Knights Templar degree. In politics he is a Democrat. He has the oldest grocery establishment now doing business in this city.

Jas. M. Reavis, Sr., member of J. M. Reavis & Son, tin, stove, glass and queensware merchants, was born July 31, 1834, in Rutherford Co., N. C., and is of a family of four sons and two daughters, born to Thos. C. and Alice (Laws) Reavis, natives of Granville and Orange Counties, N. C., father and mother respectively. They were married in Orange County, and followed farming until they moved to this county in 1834; then followed shoe-making a few years, after which he began the practice of dentistry about 1840, continuing the same in Jackson until his death in 1858, the mother following in 1871. He was city marshal of Jackson a number of years prior to his death. Our subject remained at home till 1856, when he went to New Orleans and there completed the tinner's trade, returning in 1860. He followed his trade until the beginning of hostilities between the North and South. He then enlisted, and was assigned to the engineer corps, under Forrest, remained in service until the close of the war, and in May, 1866, embarked in his present line in Jackson. In February, 1862 he married Margaret A. Brown, a native of Kentucky, to whom three sons and one daughter have been born: Frank, Alice, Hartwell and James L. Hartwell is deceased. Mr. Reavis is a member of the I. O. O. F., and his wife of the First Methodist Church.

William A. Rice, farmer, is a Henderson County Tennessean, born February 6, 1848, the tenth of eleven children born to David and Martha H. (Brooks) Rice. They were Virginians, and the father was born November 8, 1799, and came to Tennessee in 1843. He followed the life of a farmer, and died in the house in which our subject lives January 1, 1877. His wife died April 14, 1863. William A. attended the common schools, and at the age of fourteen enlisted in the Twenty-first Tennessee Cavalry, under Col. Wilson. His brother, John J. Rice, was captain of Company C, to which William belonged. He participated in the battles of Harrisburg, Springhill, Franklin and many other skirmishes and battles of less importance. While charging the rifle pits at Springhill his horse was killed under him. He surrendered at Bolivar, Tenn. He had four brothers in the army. One died in Price's army in Missouri, while acting as brigade surgeon. Capt. John J. Rice was wounded at Brice's Cross-roads and again at Harrisburg. His brother, David W., was severely wounded at Harrisburg, having been shot several times during the engagement. January 15, 1880, our subject married Lizzie Halton, daughter of William Halton, a farmer, who was killed in the machinery of a mill. Mr. and Mrs. Rice became the parents of three sons: William D., Herman and John Preston. Mrs. Rice was born in Madison County, Tenn., August 2, 1856. Mr. Rice is a Democrat, and he and wife are members of the Methodist Episcopal Church South. John J. Rice, the brother of our subject, died November 7, 1879, leaving a wife and five children. December 6, 1883, the wife died, leaving four children, one having died between the deaths of the father and mother. Our subject is now managing the estate, which consists of 1,300 acres, for the children: Mattie, Lyda Gracey, Sallie and John.

William P. Robertson, merchant of Jackson, Tenn., was born in Springfield, Washington Co., Ky., September 30, 1838, son of William and Jane (Platt) Robertson, natives, respectively, of Kentucky and Ireland. Our subject was reared to manhood in his native State, finishing his education at Transylvania University at Lexington, Ky. In 1866 he came to Jackson and established his present dry goods business in company with his present partner, John T. Botts. They employ twenty clerks in both stores, and also run a clothing store in the town. September 4, 1867, Mr. Robertson married his present wife, Miss Louanna Harris, of this city. They have five living children—three sons and two daughters—and he has one living son by his former marriage to Miss Sallie Bethel, of Kentucky. She died in 1864. Mr. Robertson is a Democrat. He has been president of the board of public schools of Jackson for the last fifteen years, and is trustee in the Southwestern Baptist University of Jackson, and is a member of the city council. He is a Knight Templar, Mason and is Past Grand Commander of the State. He is a member of the I. O. O. F. Encampment and the K. of P., and Past Grand Chancellor of the State. Himself and wife are Presbyterians. He is an elder in the church.

M. M. Robins, merchant and farmer of Pinson, Madison Co., Tenn., was born in February, 1841, in McNairy County, and is of a family consisting of twelve children, of William and Pernelia (Burton) Robins, of which our subject, two brothers and two sisters are the surviving members. North Carolina was the nativity of the parents, but in the early settlement of West Tennessee they immigrated to this part of the State and followed agricultural pursuits in McNairy and Madison Counties till their deaths, 1871 and 1883, mother and father, respectively. Our subject remained at home till the commencement of the war; then enlisted in the Thirty-first Tennessee Confederate Infantry, and served as private two years; then as orderly sergeant till captured at the battle of Missionary Ridge. He was then held till near the close of the war and exchanged, after which he returned home and farmed in McNairy County three years; then located on a farm in this county near Pinson, which he has since owned; but in 1870 he also embarked in the mercantile trade, which he continued in his country home till 1881; then became a member of the firm of Robins & Anderson, in Pinson, till 1883, at which date he bought the remaining interest and has since conducted the business alone. He owns the commodious brick store building he occupies, and carries a stock of about $4,500, consisting of general merchandise. He also owns a desirable residence in Pinson, and two farms in this county of 235 and 40 acres, respectively. In 1865 he married Mattie Tucker, a native of Madison County, to whom were born Molly (deceased), Frank E., Alice (deceased). The mother of these children died in 1871, and he afterward married Anna Johnson, to whom have been born Lee, Manly, Sheppa, Newton, Estill—all living. He is a member of the Cumberland Presbyterian Church, and politically a Democrat.

John R. Robley, a prominent grocer of Jackson, Tenn., was born in Madison County, in 1830; son of John and Elizabeth (Nanney) Robley, who were born in North Carolina, and came to Tennessee about 1829. The father was a saddler by trade, but the latter portion of his life was spent in farming. He died in 1835, and his wife in 1878. Our subject was reared on a farm and followed farming until 1877, when he started a grocery store in what was then Harrisburg, remaining there until 1880, when he located in Jackson and opened a first-class grocery, which has flourished up to the present time. In 1852 he married Ellen Black, who was born in 1837. She became the mother of seven children, three of whom are yet living. Mrs. Robley died in August, 1873, and in 1875 he married Susan Fulbright, who was born in Madison County in 1845. Husband and wife are members of the Methodist Church, and he is a member of the Masonic order, and is a stanch Democrat in politics. In

November, 1861, he enlisted in the Confederate Army, Fifty-first Tennessee Regiment, as corporal, after which he was detailed to drive an ambulance wagon. He served throughout the war, and was in some of the principal battles. The last year of the war he served under N. B. Forrest.

John T. Rone is one of the children of John and Ann (Fry) Rone, and was born in 1842. His parents were natives of North Carolina and came to Tennessee when quite young. They followed farming for a livelihood, and to them were born six children, of whom John T. is the only one now living. In 1859 the father moved to Arkansas, where he remained until his death in 1865. He died of wounds received from Federal soldiers. His wife died in 1852. The father took for his second wife Widow Palmer, who died in 1864. John T. was reared as a farmer, and went with his father to Arkansas. In May, 1861, he enlisted in the Confederate service, and thus continued honorably until the close of the war. At Kenesaw, Ga., he was slightly wounded, but returned to duty at once. He was orderly sergeant and never missed a roll-call. At the close of the war he resumed farming in this county, and has continued thus until the present. January 6, 1867, he was united in marriage with Jennie, daughter of William and Martha Blackmon. This lady was born in this county in 1842, and has presented her husband with four children—one son and three daughters. The son died in 1868, aged two years. Both parents are members of the Methodist Episcopal Church. He is a Democrat, a Mason, a Knight of the Golden Rule, and is the presiding officer of Wheeler's Lodge, No. 226. Since 1876 Mr. Rone has been justice of the peace. He has a good farm of 400 acres.

Col. Black L. Rozell was born in Maury County, August 5, 1818, and moved to Henderson County, West Tennessee, in the fall of the same year. The father and mother were natives of Maryland and North Carolina respectively. The father lived in different States until the beginning of this century, when he located in this State, and in 1831 moved to Memphis. The city was almost the daily rendezvous of the Indians, and he witnessed them crossing the Mississippi River in 1832. The father was a prosperous planter, becoming very wealthy. He died on his plantation near Memphis, in August, 1856, his wife following him in 1864. The father was eighty years of age, and the mother eighty-five. Our subject was reared on a farm, and in 1844 moved to Mississippi (being one of the judges of election when Jas. K. Polk was elected President), and engaged in farming. In 1846 he graduated in the medical college at Cincinnati, and practiced for a number of years in Mississippi, and conducted his plantation at the same time. In 1861 he was elected colonel of the Third Mississippi Regiment, remaining with them twelve months, when he received authority from headquarters to raise a regiment, which he at once proceeded to do, but after having succeeded in raising the sixth company he was taken with severe sickness, and before he could recover, his companies had been mustered into service. He then was stationed as watch on the river in Coahoma Co., and remained there till close of the war; returned to his plantation and remained until 1871, when he moved to this city, but still retains and runs his Mississippi plantation. In 1850–52 and 1854 he served in the lower house of the Mississippi State Legislature, and was nominated for the Senate for the following two years, but declined to accept. In 1882 he served the people as mayor of this city. In February, 1855, he was united in marriage to Miss Lizzie C. Lyon, of this city, and daughter of James S. Lyon. She was born in this State, August 30, 1830. He and wife are members of the Methodist Church. Mr. Rozell is in politics Democratic. He is the only surviving member of his father's family, his brother, who resided near Nashville, having died lately in his eighty-fifth year, and having been a minister for sixty-eight years.

Joel Rushing a pioneer citizen of Tennessee, was born in 1810, son of Abel and Sarah (Griffin) Rushing, who were North Carolinians and came to Tennessee in 1804. They lived in Middle Tennessee until 1819, when they came to the western portion of the State. The father was one of the hardy pioneer woodmen, and for forty years was a farmer. He was in the war of 1812, and Rushing Creek, in Benton County, derived its name from him and Willis, Dennis and Philip Rushing, they having built the first cabins in West Tennessee, on that stream. He died in 1835 and his wife in 1857. Joel Rushing has spent his entire life on a farm, and has served the people of West Tennessee in different capacities from time to time, and is, at present, coroner. He furnished two sons and a stepson for the late Confederate Army. In 1831 he married Emily Herron, of Georgia. She died in 1857, leaving ten children. In 1859 Mr. Rushing married Mrs. Sarah Prewett Vick, of Virginia, a widow of Nathan Vick, by whom she had three children. She died in 1875, and in 1876 Mr. Rushing took for his third wife, Mary Goodell, of New York State, She is a member of the Presbyterian Church, and Mr. Rushing is a Mason and Democrat.

Joel T. Rushing, chairman of the Madison County Court, was born in Henry County, in 1850. He was educated in Jackson Collége, of Jackson, Tenn., and after becoming of age learned the carpenter's trade, at which he worked about two years. He then erected a planing-mill, in which he had the misfortune to have his left hand cut off. About a year later he abandoned that business, and in 1882 was elected magistrate, which office he has held up to the present time. He was appointed trustee in May, 1886, to fill the unexpired term of a deceased trustee, and in September was elected chairman of the county court. In 1875 he married Miss Emily Smethwick, of Jackson. She is a native Tennessean, and is the mother of two children, one son and one daughter. Mr. Rushing is a Democrat, and he and wife are members of the Cumberland Presbyterian Church.

W. W. Searcy, of the firm of Searcy & McGlohn, grocers, was born in Nashville in 1846, and is the son of Dr. W. W. and Emeline (Johnson) Searcy. The parents are natives of this State. The father practiced for about fifty years in Nashville and died there in 1874, his wife preceding him in 1867. Our subject was reared in the city of Nashville, and in 1861 enlisted in the Confederate service, First Tennessee Regiment, and while engaged in battle near Vicksburg, received a wound in the right lung which rendered him unfit for duty in that regiment, so he connected himself with the Hudson Battery, Morton's brigade, under Gen. Forrest, and remained with him during the remainder of the war. In 1866 he entered the wholesale and retail grocery house of Foster Bros., remaining with them three years; then went to Cincinnati and engaged as solicitor in the cotton commission house of Cochran & Co., traveling through the States of Tennessee, Kentucky and Alabama, remaining with them one year, and went to Holly Springs, Miss., and engaged in the cotton and grocery business with Crump & Co., remaining with them five years; then came to this city and entered the hardware house of R. H. Anderson & Co. After doing business for them nine years, he purchased a half interest in the business, the style of the firm becoming Anderson & Searcy, which partnership existed until 1876, when he sold out his entire interest and connected himself with a hardware house in Nashville, making a short stay, returning to this city and engaging in his present business on the corner of Main and Shannon Streets. In 1874 he married Leonora House, of Holly Springs, Miss. She was born in Mississippi in 1853, and is the mother of four children— two daughters and two sons. He and wife are members of the Episcopal Church. In politics he is Democratic.

Nathan S. Sherman, stockholder and general manager of the Sherman man Manufacturing Company, was born in Pennsylvania in 1852, and is a son of Isaac W. and Mary P. (Pratt) Sherman. Isaac Sherman was a master mechanic, and ran the first steamboat engine shop erected in the West, over sixty years ago. Nathan S. has been a mechanic from early boyhood. He lived in Canada two years, the balance of his life being spent in Pennsylvania and New York States, before moving to Jackson, Tenn. In 1884 he opened a stock company, and has been the efficient manager of the same to the present time. In 1873 he was united in marriage to Miss Nellie M. Dewey, of Dunkirk, N. Y., and daughter of John Dewey. Three children have blessed their union—one daughter and two sons. Mr. Sherman is neutral in politics, and is considered a first-class mechanic, an excellent neighbor, and a genial, whole-souled man.

Samuel C. Simpson, a successful miller, is a native of this State; was born in 1829 to the marriage of William Simpson and Nancy Cowan. The father served in the war of 1812, and was a tanner by trade. To himself and wife were born eight children, of whom five are yet living. The father died in 1842 and his wife in 1833. After the death of his first wife he married Mrs. (Cook) Brothers, daughter of Roland Cook. This lady died in 1877. Samuel C. passed his youth at work in a tan-yard, and thoroughly understands that business in all its details, but his time has, to some extent, been occupied at other pursuits. In 1857 he engaged in the saw, grist and flouring-mill business in Tipton County, but at the end of a year started a saw-mill in Shelby County, continuing four years. In 1862 he returned to Tipton County and enlisted in the Fifty-first Tennessee Confederate Regiment, and served honorably until 1864, when he was detailed to return home for clothing, and did not again rejoin the army. He engaged in milling in Fayette County, but four years later went to Jackson and operated a saw-mill until 1877, and then came to Claybrook, where he has continued milling until the present. November 22, 1855, he married Miss Elizabeth L., daughter of William E. and Hannah (Marshall) Elmore, a native of Virginia, born in 1834. She has borne two sons and three daughters, and is a member of the Presbyterian Church. Mr. Simpson is a Democrat and a member of the Masonic order. He is a Presbyterian.

Willis R. Small was born in Henderson County, Tenn., January 13, 1836, and is the oldest of five children born to Alexander and Phœbe R. (Wilson) Small, and is of Irish descent. His father was a native of Wilson County, Tenn., and was there raised and educated. After attaining his majority he came to West Tennessee and settled in Henderson County, where he was married about 1831. He was a farmer, and died October 8, 1858. The mother was born near Raleigh, N. C., and died in Tennessee in 1864. Willis R. Small attended the common schools in his early days, and in the fall of 1861 enlisted in the Twenty-first Tennessee Cavalry, in Forrest's command. He was at Brice's Cross-roads, Memphis, Fort Pillow, Paducah and Harrisburg, and was twice wounded in the last named battle; once by a minie-ball, which passed through his liver, said to be the only case of that character where the subject survived. This disabled him for further active duty during the remainder of the war, yet he remained with his command and was surrendered at Gainesville, Ala. January 15, 1873, he was married in the house where he now lives to Susan R. Brooks, daughter of B. S. Brooks. She died November 15, 1876, leaving a daughter, Rebecca A., who was born on the 21st of August, 1876. Mr. Small is a Democrat, and his first presidential vote was cast for Seymour. He owns 360 acres of land and has a pleasant and comfortable home.

John M. Smith was born August 27, 1837, in Rutherford County, Tenn. He is the son of Capt. J. S. Smith, who was born in the same county as our subject in 1808. He married Susan Tucker, and by her became the father of one child, who died in infancy. After his wife's death he married Lucy J. Matthews, who bore him eleven children, our subject being the third of the family. In 1850 Capt. Smith immigrated to Madison County, and settled within a short distance of our subject's present home. He represented his county in the State Legislature before the war, and died in 1865. His wife was born in Williamson County, Tenn., December 7, 1813, and died in Madison County September 22, 1880. Their son, John M. Smith, received good early educational advantages. At the breaking out of the war he joined the Sixth Tennessee Infantry, under Col. William H. Stevens, and participated in the battles of Perryville, Ky., Murfreesboro, Missionary Ridge, and was in the famous retreat from Dalton to Atlanta. He was married in Madison County, October 20, 1858, to Ruth A. Vann, daughter of James R. Vann. To their union were born Mary E., James A. and Susan T. Mary and James died on the same day, December 26, 1875. Mrs. Smith was born in Madison County, August 25, 1840. Our subject is a Democrat, and owns 255 acres of land, on which he raises a diversity of crops, but gives his chief attention to cotton and corn.

J. C. Smith, owner and manager of the Jackson Foundry and Machine Works, was born in Jefferson County, Tenn., in 1846, and is the son of J. C. and C. K. (Moser) Smith. Our subject was reared to manhood in the town of Newmarket, and received his education in the Holston College of the same town. In early life he was very desirous of becoming a railroad employe, and soon obtained the position of newsboy on a railroad, selling papers to Confederate soldiers, which he followed for some time, and then was employed as conductor, of which position he well discharged the duties until 1868, when he located in this city. He then entered into the merchandise business, which proved successful until he closed out, in 1879, for the purpose of engaging in his present work. After closing in 1879, he at once purchased the old Madison foundry, and gave it a thorough reconstruction, which makes it at present equal to any similar establishment in the South, and is thoroughly equipped for executing any kind of work in his line on short notice. In 1872 he was united in marriage to Miss Emma Wright, of Florence, Ala., daughter of James Wright. To this union have been born four children, two males and two females. Our subject's wife was born in 1854, and is a member of the Presbyterian Church. Our subject is a Mason in good standing, and a Democrat in politics.

Erasmus D. Sneed, a good citizen of this county, was born in Madison County, Miss., August 8, 1849. The father, Albert Sneed, was born in North Carolina, and went to Mississippi in 1832. He was a life-long farmer, and supported a family of thirteen children—four daughters, and nine sons—five of whom are living. The mother, Maria F. Bullock, was born in North Carolina. The parents were members of the Episcopal Church. The father died in 1874, his wife preceding him about one year. Our subject was reared to manhood on the farm, then railroaded a while, after which he engaged in the mercantile business, at Canton, Miss., and in 1873 came to Claybrook, this county, and after doing business there for three years, moved to Jackson, where he has continued business up to the present time. He has moved on his farm, and directs his attention to it exclusively, his mercantile business being run by partner. In 1877 he married Miss Alice R. Lanier, daughter of J. H. and Casander (Barham) Lanier. She was born in 1856, and is the mother of six children; three daughters and one son are living; twins died in infancy. He is a member of the Episcopal Church, and his wife a member of the Methodist Church. He is a member of the K. of H., and in politics he is Democratic.

John T. Stark, present recorder of the city of Jackson, was born in Tennessee, December 1, 1848, and is the son of Robert and Emeline (Moore) Stark. The parents are natives of Ireland and South Carolina, respectively, the mother being reared in the city of Philadelphia. The father came to the United States while yet a young man; located in Philadelphia where he married, then came to Tennessee, where he lived until his death, which occurred in 1854, his wife following him in 1863. The father was a merchant tailor by trade, and was moderately successful through life. He held the office of mayor of this city for some years, and also was deputy county clerk for some time. Our subject was born in this city, and is living in the house of his birth; after the war he went to Paducah, Ky., where he engaged as clerk in a drug store, and where he remained for some months, then returned to his native city, and entered the position of deputy clerk, in the county clerk's office, under P. O. McCowat, which position he honorably filled for about seven years, being there in 1875, after which he was elected to his present office, and has faithfully discharged the duties up to the present time. In 1873 he was united in marriage to Miss Ella S. Barton, of Milam County, Tex., who is the mother of two children—Barton and Robert F.; Robert F. died in 1879, in his third year. Subject and wife are members of St. Luke's Episcopal Church. He is a member of the I. O. O. F., K. of H. and K. of P. In politics he is strictly Democratic.

Wilson E. Stewart, a prominent farmer of Madison County, was born April 13, 1821, in Montgomery County, N. C., one of nine children born to Shadrack and Mary (Hurrey) Stewart, of which our subject, one brother and four sisters are the surviving members. The parents were natives of North Carolina, and were married there. They farmed a few years in that State, and in 1836 came to Tennessee, locating in McNairy County, where they resided, farming until their deaths in 1857 and 1859, respectively. Our subject remained at home until 1848. He then married and followed agricultural pursuits several years. For six years he was in the merchandise business in McNairy County, and at the close of the war he accepted a clerkship in Pinson, which position he filled two years, and in 1869 located on his present home tract of 120 acres, one and one-half miles southwest of Pinson. He also has 186 acres in another tract in the county. His first wife was Jane E. Bostick, a native of Madison County. She bore him four children, of whom two are still living. She died in 1857, and in 1859 he married Margaret C. Bostick. By this wife he had two children, one, a son, still living. She died in 1862, and in 1868 he married Mary Alexander *nee* Pickens, to whom one child, a daughter, has been born, and is still living. This lady had two children by her first husband, one, a son, surviving. Subject is a Democrat, and a member of the F. & A. M., and with his family is a member of the Methodist Church.

H. H. Swink, of the firm of Swink Bros., was born in Tennessee in 1841, and is the son of P. J. and Malinda Swink. The parents are natives of North Carolina, and came to Tennessee in 1836. The father was a merchant, yet successfully followed farming also. He died in 1851. Our subject was reared to the age of fifteen years on the farm, when he, in partnership with Z. Voss, opened a grocery in this town, and did business up to the commencement of the war. Our subject then enlisted in the Confederate service, Thirteenth Tennessee Regiment, under Col. Neely, and remained until wounded at Yazoo City, in March, 1863, which so disabled him that he was compelled to remain at home. During the remainder of the war he worked at the saddler's trade, and at the close resumed the grocery business, in which he continued up to the present time, having added largely to his stock, dry goods, clothing and hardware. In 1876 his brother, Geo. W., went in partnership with him, the firm being known as Swink Bros. Our subject was married in 1873 to Miss Sallie Williams, of this county, daughter of John H. Williams. She was born in 1850, and is the mother of six children, three daughters and three sons. He is a Democrat, and a member of the Masonic order.

Taylor Bros. are lumber dealers of Jackson, Tenn., and the firm is composed of M. H. and W. A. Taylor, who established their business March 1, 1886. Wyatt A. Taylor, their father, was born in Wayne County, N. C., November 18, 1833, son of Mark and Nancy A. (Altman) Taylor, both of whom were North Carolinians. They came to Tennessee about 1839, and here Wyatt A. was reared to manhood. He attended the common schools in boyhood, and followed agricultural pursuits very successfully until the war, when he enlisted in the Fifty-first Tennessee Regiment under Johnston. After the battle of Shiloh he joined Forrest's cavalry and served two years as a private. He was wounded twice during the time. Since that date he has resided in Jackson, and up to 1872 was engaged in the mercantile business. Since that time he has followed trading in real estate, live stock, etc., and has also given personal supervision to his two plantations. In 1858 he married Tennessee V. Collins, who died in 1872, having borne him four sons and four daughters, Mark H. and William A., lumber dealers of Jackson, being of the number. Mr. Taylor next married Elvira Lawrence, and their marriage resulted in the birth of two sons. This wife died in 1877, and in 1878 he married his present wife, who was Mary Emma (Wilson) Allen, of Vicksburg, Miss. They have two sons and one daughter. Mr. Taylor is a Democrat, and belongs to the Masonic and K. of H. fraternities. He and Mrs. Taylor are members of the Methodist Episcopal Church. Mrs. Taylor was a teacher in the Main Street High School of Vicksburg, Miss., at the time of her marriage to Mr. Wyatt A. Taylor, and had been teaching in that school for seven years previous to her marriage.

Atha Thomas was born in Madison County, December 28, 1833, and is the son of John P. Thomas, who was born in Franklin County, N. C., in 1804, and immigrated to Tennessee in 1825, locating in this county. He here married Marina, daughter of Benjamin Boone. To these parents was born a family of six sons and two daughters, our subject being the third child. The father followed agricultural pursuits chiefly, and died at the home of our subject June 20, 1882. The mother was born in

North Carolina in 1812, and was brought to Tennessee when fifteen years of age. She died in this county April 15, 1846. Atha, in youth, was fairly well educated and chose the occupation of farming. When the late war broke out he enlisted in the Sixth Tennessee Confederate Infantry Regiment, and during his active term of service participated gallantly in the battles of Perryville, Murfreesboro, Chickamauga and also the Georgia campaign. At Dalton he was promoted to second lieutenant, and held that commission until the end of the war. From Shiloh until he was made lieutenant he was second sergeant. In 1864 he did provost duty at Macon, Ga., and after Hood's Tennessee campaign joined his force. At the time of the surrender he was at home on furlough. February 2, 1860, he married Miss Lucinda, daughter of William Blackmon. Eight children are the results of this union, six living: Martha M. (Raines), James J., Tennie J., Robert A., Lizzie P. and Claudie B. Mrs. Thomas was born in Gibson County, November 18, 1840. Mr. Thomas is a Democrat, and he, his wife and four children are members of the Methodist Episcopal Church South. His farm of 230 acres lies ten miles northeast of Jackson.

John L. H. Tomlin, attorney at law of Jackson, Tenn., was born in Isle of Wight County, Va., September 5, 1826, and is the son of Matthew and Frances (Holcombe) Tomlin, both natives of the Old Dominion State. The father removed to Tennessee after the mother's death about 1828. He located in Madison County, where he conducted a plantation successfully until his death, August 12, 1862. Our subject was reared to manhood in this county, securing a good education in the common schools and West Tennessee College, of this city. In his nineteenth year he began the study of law, with a view to making it a profession for life. So he accordingly entered the law office of J. D. McClellan, of Jackson, with whom he read law, and finally entered into practice with him in 1845, and continued until Mr. McClellan's death. Mr. Tomlin has ever since been engaged in the practice at Jackson, having met with more than ordinary and well deserved success. May 19, 1846, he married Amanda C. Elder, of Gibson County, Tenn., who died in November, 1852, leaving four children: Ella F., the widow of R. S. Lindsey; Horace W.; Eliza, the wife of J. T. Botts, and Mary L., the wife of James M. Houston, of St. Louis. July 5, 1866, he was married in Mobile, Ala., to Miss Elvira B. Hurt. They have one child—Sarah Eunice. Mr. Tomlin is a conservative Democrat in his political views, but was formerly an old line Whig. He never aspired to political prominence. He was United States pension agent under President Fillmore, and made the race for the chancery court judgeship in 1878. He has been mayor of Jackson several terms, and altogether has taken an active and leading interest in all public and private enterprises. He has also been city attorney of Jackson, Tenn. He is a member of the I. O. O. F. (Encampment). Himself and wife are leading members of the Presbyterian Church, of which he is an elder. He has also been the efficient superintendent of the Presbyterian Sunday-school for the past thirty years in this city.

Robert A. Treadwell, a prominent citizen of Jackson, Tenn., was born in Rutherford County, N. C., August 18, 1831, and is the son of Timmons L. and Eliza (Allison) Treadwell, both natives of the Carolinas. Our subject removed with his parents in 1836 to northern Mississippi, where he was reared to manhood. In 1858 he engaged in the mercantile business in Memphis, and continued until the war, when he enlisted in Company A, Seventh Tennessee Confederate Cavalry Regiment, serving four years, or until the close. He then resumed business in northern Mississippi, and in 1869 returned to Memphis, and conducted business successfully until 1872, when he came to Jackson and engaged in the mercantile business, continuing four years. He then devoted his attention to agricultural pursuits, and has conducted a large plantation in the county ever since, and for the last four years has been engaged in railroad contracting. In 1869 he married Susan M., daughter of the late Col. Wm. H. Long. Three children have been the result of this union, all of whom are living: Wm. L., Elizabeth A. and Robert A. Politically Mr. Treadwell is a Democrat, and justly recognized as one of Jackson's most enterprising and successful citizens.

James M. Trotter, proprietor of the book and stationery establishment of this city, was born in this State in 1858, and is the son of George W. and Sallie E. (Merriweather) Trotter. The parents are also natives of this State. The father was a very prosperous cotton merchant of Memphis, having met with reverses about 1868, which embarrassed him to some extent. The mother died in 1860. Our subject was reared in this city by his aunt, his mother having died when he was eighteen months old. He was one of the first graduates of the Southwestern Baptist University, of this city. He read law for three years, and practiced the same for two years, after which he engaged with the Hartford Life & Annuity Insurance Company, remaining with them two years; then engaged in his present business, which he has made popular and profitable, and which was established in 1883. In 1883 he was united in marriage to Miss Beulah B. Bright, of this city, and daughter of James E. and Josephine (Sanders) Bright. She was born in Arkansas in 1861. He and wife are members of the First Presbyterian Church. In politics he is a stanch Democrat.

Job Umphlett, undertaker and dealer in furniture, at Jackson, Tenn., was born in Gates County, N. C., February 21, 1827; son of Lewis and Mahala (Russell) Umphlett, who were born in North Carolina and Virginia, respectively. Job Umphlett was reared and educated in his native State, and spent one year in the Mexican war, under Jefferson Davis, in Company K, Tombigbee Volunteers. In 1853 he came to Jackson, where he was engaged in the manufacture of carriages until the breaking out of the war. He then organized Company C, Thirty-eighth Regiment, Confederate Infantry, and served as captain of his company until the reorganization of the army in 1862. He was rendered unfit for military duty for about one year, owing to sickness, and then attached himself to Forrest's cavalry, and served until the close of the war. He then farmed successfully in Madison County until 1872, and the following four years was in the lumber business. From that time until October, 1886, he was in the undertaking business with W. D. Robinson. In September, 1885, he had started the furniture business, and has conducted these combined enterprises very successfully. October 11, 1855, he married Mirham S. Collins, of Henderson County, Tenn. They have one child living—Lewis C. Mr. Umphlett is a Democrat in politics, and is a Royal Arch Mason, and is a member of the K. of H., and K. G. R. He and family are members of the Methodist Episcopal Church.

Joseph W. Wallace, register of Madison County, was born in Edgecomb County, N. C., October 1, 1830, the son of Warren and Mourning (Raspberry) Wallace, both of whom were natives of North Carolina. The father came to Tennessee in 1831, locating in Hardin County, on the Tennessee River, where himself and wife spent the remainder of their lives. They were most exemplary citizens. Joseph W. was reared as a farmer, securing a fair education, and preparing himself for teaching, which occupation he followed irregularly from 1845 until 1882. In 1853 he went to Arkansas, but returned to Hardin County in 1860, and when the war broke out enlisted early in 1862 in Company G, Fifth Kentucky Confederate Regiment, and was captured at Baton Rouge, La., August 5, 1862, and was held a prisoner of war until the following October. In November, 1862, he was transferred to the Twenty-third Tennessee Battalion, and was promoted at Chickamauga to color-bearer, and served as such until August 19, 1864, at Atlanta, where he lost his left leg (and was held as a prisoner of war until March 9, 1865), when he retired on full pay. After the war he returned to Hardin County, but soon left there and followed his profession, and in 1870 came to Madison County, where he has since resided, following book-selling and teaching, and in 1882 was elected to his present position of register. His re-election in

1886 attests his popularity. August 12, 1851, Mr. Wallace married Sarah A. Gage, who died March 3, 1859, leaving two children: Cynthia J., widow of J. W. Allison, and Sarah E., wife of J. L. Allison. December 10, 1865, he married his present wife, Margaret Ann Lewis, who has borne her husband three living children: Robert H. Lee, Florence H. and Jennie B. Mr. Wallace is a Democrat, and he and wife are members of the Methodist Episcopal Church South, he having joined the same in 1847.

Samuel H. Wallace was born in White County, Tenn., on the 5th of June, 1851. His father, Matthew H. Wallace, was of Scotch extraction, and descended from the celebrated Wallace family of Scotland. He was born in Jackson County, Tenn., in 1807, and after attaining his majority moved to White County, where he married Mary E. Hampton, a cousin of Wade Hampton, of South Carolina. In 1868 he moved to Marshall County, and in 1874 to Madison County, settling in the eastern portion. To him and wife were born eight sons and two daughters, our subject being the fourth member of the family. Matthew Wallace was twice married, having five children by his first wife. The father was a farmer, and died in August, 1883. His wife was born in Rutherford County, N. C., in 1824, and is still living at the old homestead. Samuel H. received a liberal English education, and has followed dairying and farming as his chief business through life. He began doing for himself at the age of nineteen, and by industry and economy became the owner of 170 acres of land. He was married in Madison County September 30, 1873, to Mary J. Nelson, daughter of Noah Nelson, and by her is the father of the following children: Johnnie L., Beulah E., James H., Thomas A., Jessie Iva and Barbara Edna. Mrs. Wallace was born in Madison County, Tenn., January 31, 1857. Mr. Wallace is a Democrat, and his first presidential vote was cast for Samuel J. Tilden. He is also a member of the K. of H.

F. W. Watlington, merchant, farmer and postmaster, of Pinson, Tenn., was born November 7, 1835, in Madison County, and is one of a family consisting of five sons and three daughters, of George and Catharine (Tabler) Watlington, of which our subject, four brothers and one sister, are the surviving members. The parents were natives of Dinwiddie County, Va., and were married there, but soon after came to Tennessee, locating at first near Knoxville, but after a few years came to this county. About 1830 they located near Pinson, where they engaged in agricultural pursuits till their deaths, in 1863 and 1866, mother and father respectively. Our subject remained at home till the death of his parents; then, in 1867, he married Mary J. Anderson, a native of this county. He then followed the carpenter's trade a few years, after which he followed farming till 1873, when he moved to Pinson and embarked in the mercantile trade, which he' has since successfully followed. To Mr. and Mrs. Watlington one child, a son, Wm. F., has been born, who is at present connected with his father in his store, and is one of Pinson's most promising young men. Mr. Watlington has a tract of 300 acres of land near Pinson, and a residence in the village; also a part interest in the large brick store building he occupies. He has been a justice of the peace and a notary public of his district several years. He is a member of the F. & A. M., and he and family are members of the Methodist Church.

John T. Whitehead, proprietor of the City Marble Works, was born in Boston, England, in 1840, and was taken to Canada by his father in 1847. His parents, James and Susanna (Carter) Whitehead, were born in England, and the father was a glover by trade, and died in Canada in 1855. His wife died about 1853. In 1857 John T. Whitehead went to Holly Springs, Miss., where he was engaged in the marble business. In 1861 he enlisted in the Confederate service—First Tennessee Heavy Artillery, and served until taken prisoner in the fall of 1862, at Island No. 10. He made his escape immediately after his capture, and returned to the army. He was soon after captured and paroled at Vicksburg, and was again captured shortly afterward by Gen. Sherman, but succeeded in effecting his escape. While at Fort Morgan, in Mobile Bay, he was taken prisoner for the fourth time, and retained eleven months in a military prison. He first began serving as lieutenant, and was made captain of artillery. After the close of the war he went to Toledo, Ohio, where he worked at his trade until 1869; then again came South, locating at Holly Springs, where he remained until 1879. Since that time he has resided in Jackson, and has a first-class marble trade. He met with quite severe reverses while at Holly Springs, his losses amounting to about $10,000. In 1876 he was married to Rhoda A. Boden, of Toledo, Ohio, and daughter of Samuel and Mary-Ette Boden. Mrs. Whitehead was born in Indiana about 1848, and is the mother of four children: Luella M., Herbert B., Katie Almira and William T. L. Mr. Whitehead is a Democrat and Mason, and has taken all the degees of that order, including the Knights Templar degree. He and wife are members of the Episcopal Church.

Nolan S. White, president of the Bank of Madison, at Jackson, Tenn., a native of Montgomery County, Tenn., was born December 28, 1839, son of Willie S. and Lucy W. (Sherman) White, both natives of Virginia. Subject's father died when he was but three or four years of age, and the mother removed to Baton Rouge, La., where Nolan S. was reared and educated. At the age of fourteen he began clerical work at New Orleans, later in Memphis, where he became paying teller of the Bank of Memphis. Upon the breaking out of war he went to Chattanooga, from where he enlisted in the Confederate service, serving as private in the Bluff City Greys, of Memphis, until the close of the war. After the war he resumed the banking business in Memphis, and June 6, 1866, came to Jackson and organized the Bank of Madison, accepting the position of cashier, and about 1870 became its president, and has served faithfully and efficiently in this capacity to the present time. August 15, 1882, he married Mary De Lesseleine Perkins, his present wife. Two children— one son and one daughter—are the fruits of this union. Mr. White is an unswerving Democrat, a member of the K. of P., K. of H. and A. O. U. W. Himself and wife are members of the Episcopal Church. Mr. White is also prominently identified with various other business enterprises in Jackson, being a stockholder in oil-mills, woolen-mills, ice factory and gas works, and is recognized as one of the most enterprising and reliable business men and citizens of Jackson. Mr. White first married Maria Mason, of this county, who died October, 1872.

H. L. White, of the firm of H. L. White & Bro., was born in Tennessee in 1842, and is the son of A. M. and Harriet B. (Bryant) White. The father was a farmer, and died in this county in 1879. Our subject was reared on a farm, and remained until 1879, when he moved to this city, and engaged in the grocery business, which he continued for four years; then sold out and traded in real estate and cotton until a few months since, when he, in partnership with his brother, erected a cotton-gin in this city, and have it in good running condition. In 1862 he enlisted in the Confederate service, remaining about ten months, but being sick most of the time, returned home. In 1876 he married Miss E. F. Glenn, of this county, and daughter of H. C. and Elizabeth Glenn. She was born in this State in 1857, and is the mother of four children—two daughters and two sons; one son and one daughter are dead. He and wife are members of the Baptist Church, and in politics he is Democratic.

Lilleon W. Whitaker, a prominent druggist of Jackson, was born in Goldsboro, N. C., in 1859, and is the son of L. F. and Almyra (Randolph) Whitaker. The parents are natives of North Carolina. In 1866 the mother died, and in 1871 the father came to this State. His second wife, to whom he was married in 1868, was Rowena Oates. The father was a professor of music, and at present lives at Sandersville, Ga. Our subject is one of eleven children, and spent his boyhood in the town of Goldsboro, beginning life for himself at the age of twelve years. He worked three years in a printing office, and then entered a drug store continuing until 1883, when he began the same business for himself, and has thus continued until the present, meeting with satisfactory success. In 1880 he was united in marriage with Miss Lillie, daughter of John J. and Eliza Williams, who was born in this State in 1860, and is the mother of three children—one son and two daughters. He and wife are members of St. Luke's Episcopal Church. He is a member of the K. of H., and in politics is a stanch Democrat.

Robert B. Williams, senior member of the firm of Williams & Perry, boot and shoe dealers, North Lafayette Street, Jackson, was born in May, 1844, in Pittsylvania County, Va., and one of a family of eight children born to John H. and Jane M. (Gardner) Williams, of which our subject and three sisters are the surviving members. The father was a native of Virginia, the mother of North Carolina. They were married in Virginia and farmed there a few years, then came to this county in 1844. The father continued farming till 1865, then embarked in the mercantile line at Medon, this county, in which he continued three years, then came to Jackson, continuing in the same business till his death, which occurred May, 1870, the mother following in 1880. Our subject remained with his parents until 1876, then married Lula O. Grant, of Maury County, Tenn., a native of Virginia. In 1864 he enlisted in the Twenty-first Confederate Cavalry, remaining a few months, then returned home. Soon after his father's death he accepted a clerkship with F. H. Mayo, of Jackson, and continued with him about seven years. He then embarked in the dry goods trade under the firm name of Williams & Day, continued two years, then accepted clerkship with W. D. Dowdy & Bro. He remained with them till November, 1881, then acted as traveling salesman one year and returned to F. H. Mayo, remaining with him till March 10, 1886. From that date until September 15, of the same year, he dealt in boots, shoes, umbrellas, trunks and hats, under the business name of Williams' Boot & Shoe Store. At the last named date Williams & Perry succeeded to the business. His wife, referred to above, died June 15, 1882, and in September, 1884, he married Mrs. M. H. Crim, nee Perry. He and wife are members of the Baptist Church. He is a Democrat, and a member of the K. of H.

Thomas T. Wilson, carpenter and contractor, was born in McNairy County, March 9, 1851, son of George D. Wilson, who was born in Guilford County, N. C., and immigrated to Tennessee in about 1840. He was married three times; the first time in North Carolina, and the last two times in McNairy County, Tenn. Our subject was one of seven children born to the third marriage. The first marriage resulted in one son and three daughters. The father was a cabinet-maker and farmer and was at one time greatly interested in the construction of the Mobile & Ohio Railroad, He died at the old homestead in McNairy County, March 20, 1860. . The mother was born in Montgomery County, N. C., and died at Bethel, November 4, 1870, at the age of sixty. Thomas T. Wilson was reared on a farm and obtained a limited education in the common schools, but by personal application at a later period he succeeded in acquiring a good business education. From 1871 until about 1873 he followed merchandising, and during the next two years attended college at Purdy and at Bethel, Tenn. The last seven years have been spent in carpentering and contracting, and he is now engaged in that business in Jackson, Tenn. He was married in Hardeman County, Tenn., April 4, 1880, to Jennie L. Crawford, daughter of I. W. Crawford. Of three children born to them, but one is living—Wilford D., who was born March 11, 1881. Mrs. Wilson was born in Hardeman County in 1856. Mr. Wilson is a Democrat, and a member of the K. of L.

William B. Wilie, trustee of Madison County, was born May 28, 1831, being the son of James and Martha (Doake) Wilie, both natives of North Carolina. The father came to this State in 1819, locating in Wilson County, and in 1829 came to Madison County, and followed farming until his death in 1866. He was an exemplary citizen and lived to a ripe old age, dying in his eighty-third year. William B. was reared and educated in this county, and at the age of twenty-three years left the farm and engaged in the mercantile business with his brother at Huntersville, now Anderson Chapel, of this county. In 1860 he entered the service of the Pioneer Express Company, running on the Mobile & Ohio Railroad during the early part of the war, remaining in this service at different places until 1866. He then farmed until 1878, when he was made deputy sheriff, serving six years. In 1886 he was elected trustee. In 1879 he married Miss Eliza G. Alexander, and one child, Lillie May, has blessed this union. Mr. Wilie is a faithful Democrat, and in religious faith he and wife are Presbyterians. He is one of the most substantial citizens of the county.

Christopher Columbus Williams, a prominent citizen of this county, was born in Tennessee in 1855, and is the son of Porter and Mary A. (Billington) Williams. The parents are natives of this State. The father is a life-long farmer, and supported a family of eleven children, eight by his first wife and three by the second. The mother died in 1876. In 1878 he married Nancy Barker, who became the mother of the three children. Our subject was reared on a farm, and has followed it all his life. In 1878 he married Miss C. A. Lanier, daughter of J. H.

and Casander (Barham) Lanier. She was born in this State in 1850, and is the mother of three children—two daughters and one son; one daughter died in 1885. He and wife are members of the Methodist Church. In politics he is strictly Democratic.

Joseph J. Worrell, editor and proprietor of the Jackson *Despatch*, is a native of Hardeman County, and was born November 19, 1843, to the marriage of John Worrell and Harriett Williams, both of whom were natives of North Carolina. The father came to Tennessee in 1833, locating in Hardeman County, where he farmed until late in life, when he moved to the adjoining county of Fayette, where both parents died. Joseph J. grew to the age of seventeen years on a farm, receiving only an ordinary education. When the war broke out, at the age of seventeen he enlisted in the One Hundred and Fifty-fourth Senior Tennessee Confederate Regiment, and was assigned to Gen. Cheatham's division. He served three years as a private, and after the war engaged in mercantile pursuits two years in Somerville, Fayette County, and clerked in the same business two years in Memphis. In 1872 he came to Jackson and engaged in the newspaper business as solicitor, and in August, 1873, he and A. H. Parker, established the Jackson *Despatch*, and three months after, Mr. Worrell bought his partner's interest, and has since conducted the paper alone. This venture, a difficult one at any time, has been highly successful. The paper represents clean and pure Democracy, and is the champion of the people's rights. His paper was the first to advocate the nomination of R. L. Taylor for governor of Tennessee. February 18, 1875, Mr. Worrell was united in marriage with Miss Lua G. Taylor, of Jackson, Tenn., and to this union there are two living children: Sallie Lula and Kate. Mr. Worrell is a member of the K. of H., and is a progressive thinker and an enterprising business man.

John R. Young, farmer and miller, was born in this county, September 3, 1851. His father, John Young, was also a native of this county and was born December 28, 1823. He was here reared and educated and upon reaching his majority was united in marriage with Mary J., daughter of Parks Chandler. Great-grandfather Young was a native of Ireland, and came to America during the Revolution, and immediately enlisted in the cause of the colonies, continuing until peace was declared. John R. is the third in a family of four sons and two daughters. The father was a mill-wright, but followed farming also, and died September 19, 1884. The mother was born in Madison County and is still living. John R. grew to man's estate on the farm, receiving in youth a liberal education, finishing at West Tennessee College, at Jackson. Mr. Young has been chiefly employed in milling. He was in business in Jackson two years. He is now interested in two grist-mills, one saw-mill and one cotton-gin, the entire plant costing about $10,000. He was married in Gibson County, May 3, 1877, to Miss Oraella, daughter of L. G. B. Seat, and three children are the results of this union: Myrtle, John R. and Ernest. The mother was born in Gibson County, July 16, 1856. Mr. Young is a Democrat, a Mason (member of St. John's Lodge, No. 332, at Jackson), and owns 445 acres. He is a Methodist, and his wife a Missionary Baptist. His grandfather, James Young, was a mill-wright, and a native of Henry County, Tenn., and died in Arkansas about the year 1857.

Daniel P. York, a prominent citizen of this city, was born in Kentucky, in 1828, and is the son of James and Elizabeth (Parker) York. The parents were natives of Kentucky, and came to Tennessee in 1831, bringing our subject with them. The father was a farmer and stock raiser by occupation, and was very prosperous in life, and to himself and wife were born three daughters and one son. He was in the war of 1812. The father died in 1836, his wife preceding him about three years. Our subject was reared to the age of sixteen on a farm, when he engaged as clerk in a dry goods and grocery store at Medon, in this county, remaining until the partnership expired, then clerked for Dr. Bates in Bolivar, for a short time, after which he returned to this city, and later accepted a position with Price & Hess, peddling clocks and dry goods in the northern portion of this State, remaining with them about five years. On the 1st of January, 1851, he was united in marriage to Miss Sarah E. Barham, of Carroll County, this State, and daughter of Thos. and Sarah Barham. She was born in this State in 1830, and is the mother of one child named James R. Immediately after marriage he began farming in Carroll County, and remained until 1862, when he enlisted in the Confederate service, in the Sixteenth Tennessee Regiment, remaining with them through the entire war. He received two flesh wounds—one while at Harrisburg, and one at the battle of Franklin. After the war he returned to Carroll County and remained two years, then came to this city and engaged in the butchering and market business. A few months since he sold out, and directs his attention to buying and shipping stock. He and wife and son are members of the First Methodist Church. He is a Master Mason, and in politics he is strictly Democratic.

J. W., 804
JOHN W., 815
ROBERT, 859
W. B., 807
W. W., 886
W. W., COL.,
  815, 845
GATES & ENLOE, 815

GAYLE,
  PETER S., REV.,
  831
  REV., 831
  S. J., 817
GENTRY,
  GEORGE, 800
GHOLSON,
  BENJAMIN, 803
GIBBS,
  A. F., 817
  F. G., 822
  GEN., 823
GILBERT,
  J. A., 817
GILES,
  CALVIN, 847
  MAGGIE E., 847
GILKIN,
  S. F., 810
GILLESPIE,
  BENJAMIN, 821
GILLIKIN,
  JAMES, 862
  LUCINDA
  (DUNCAN), 862
  SAMUEL F., 862
GILMORE,
  H. B., 814
GLASS,
  THOMAS E., 832
GLASS & SON, 810
GLEN,
  HENRY, 822
GLENN,
  E. F., 913
  ELIZABETH, 913
  H. C., 913
  JAMES R., DR.,
  868
  LIZZIE W., 868
GLOVER,
  MAJ., 869
GOLDEN,
  FOSTER, 799
  RICHARD, 799
GOOCH,
  ANGUS, 863
  ARTHUR M., 862
  EUNICE, 863
  EVA E., 863
  FLORENCE E., 863
  GEORGE R., 862
  HATTIE L., 862
  J. C., CAPT.,
  862(2)

JAMES T., 862
ROWLAND, 862
RUFUS C., 862
S. P., 863
GOODELL,
  MARY, 901
GOODWIN,
  A. B., 822
GORDON,
  ELIZABETH C.,
  863
  W. W., 863
GORMAN, 810
GOURLEY,
  BEN F., 825
GRANT,
  LULA O., 914
GRAVES,
  J. R., REV., 831
  JOHN, 819
GRAY,
  ARTHUR F., 804
  BALYS E., 863
  E. D., 863
  H. L., 800, 804
  H. W., 804
  S. F., 808
  SARAH E.
  (WITHERS), 863
GREELEY,
  HORACE, 893
GREEN,
  ALEX P., 825
  J. C., 811
  J.C., 812
  WM. M., RT.
  REV., 835
GREENBERRY,

  —, 805
GREER,
  ALEXANDER, 864

  DELIA E., 864
  HENRIETTA E.,
  864
  J. M., 822
  JAMES, 800, 834
  JAMES N., 863,
  864
  JOHN A., 814,
  864
  MARGARET
  (SPRATT), 864
  NEOPHLET A., 864

  ROBERT L., 864
  VIRGINIA C., 864
GRIFFINS,
  —, 825
  THOMAS, 825
GRIFFITH,
  W. R., 810
GRIFFORD,
  J., 816

GUINN,
  ANDREW J., 864
  JOHN, 864
GUTHRIE,
  ANDREW, 807

-H-

HACKNEY,
  JAMES, 865
  JOSEPH D., 865
  KEZIAH (DAVIS),

  865
HALE,
  —, 825
  WYLEY POPE, 825

HALEY & BRO., 810

HALL,
  A. C., 822
  A. J., REV., 831
  ARCHIBALD C.,
  820
  R. W., 858
  SALLIE T., 858
HALTON,
  B., 826
  LIZZIE, 898
  WILLIAM, 898
HAMILTON,
  J. R., REV., 831
HAMMERLY,
  JOSEPH, 865
  RICHARD H., 865
  VIRGINIA B.
  (NOEL), 865
HAMMOND,
  ELIZ.
  R.(MORGAN)(POWEL

  L), 866
  IVA R., 866
  JAMES, 866
  LEIGH, 866
  M. M., 810
  MAUDE C., 866
  MILES M., 866
  WALTER, 866
  WILLIAM, 866
HAMNER,
  R. M., 810
HAMPTON,
  MARY E., 911
  W. F., 835
  WADE, 911
HANAMER,
  LOIS, 805
HANCOCK,
  —, 852
  GEN., 868
HANEY,
  D. R., 813
HARALSON,

HERNDON, 802,
  803, 804, 808,
  809, 819
  VINCENT, 800,
  804(2), 808(2),
  818
HARDAGE,
  J. M., 807
HARDEMAN,
  T. J., 801
HARDGROVE,
  JOHN, 799, 803,
  818
HARMON,
  JOHN, 839
HARPER,
  EDWARD, 866
  FANNIE, 830
  J. H., 812(3),
  813, 827
  JESSE H., 866
  MARTHA
  (HANCOCK), 866
  WILLIAM, 800
HARPER'S
  INSTITUTE, 867
HARRIS, 810
  B. R., 813,
  817(2)
  BENJAMIN R.,
  DR., 868
  EDWARD W., 868
  G. N., 810
  GOV., 849
  J. C., 868
  J. W., 807, 823
  JULIUS C.,
  868(2)
  LOUANNA, 898
  MARIA W.
  (BRIGGS), 868
  MARY S., 868
  SUSAN C.
  (SMITH), 868
  WALTER S.,
  868(2)
  WESLEY, 868
  WILLIAM, 868
  WM., 800, 807
HARRIS & WARD, 810
HARRISON,
  —, 804
  DR., 835
  EMMA, 842
  JAMES, 813, 842
  JOHN, 804
  JOHN A., REV.,
  835
  W. H., 818
  WM., 800
HART,
  ROBERT, 813
HARTON,
  H., 809
HASKELL,

NEEDHAM,
  LEWIS, 818
  MOSES, 800
NEELEY,
  DR., 809
  J. C., 805
  J. J., COL., 826
  THOMAS, REV.,
    833
NEELY,
  COL., 906
  DR., 817, 837
  M. S., 810
NEILL,
  MARGARET, 850

NELSON,
  —, 810
  A., DR., 824
  COL., 891
  MARTHA
    (HENDERSON), 890

  MARY J., 911
  NOAH, 911
  W.T., 814(2)
  WILLIAM D., 890,
    891
  WILLIAM T., 890,
    891
NEWBERN,
  JOE, 832
NEWELL,
  ----, 833
  S. W., 834
NEWLY,
  ALICE, 896
NEWMAN,
  C. G., 817
NEWSOM,
  —, 801
  COL., 838
  LEWIS, 833
  WM., 820
NEWSON,
  —, 801
  J. M. (COL.),
    847
NICHOLS,
  WILLIAM, 820
NICKS,
  WM., 825
NORVELL,
  JOHN R., 835
  THOMAS G., 835
NORVILL,
  JOHN, 805
NORVILLE,
  JOHN, 803
  THOMAS, 803
NORWOOD,
  J. W., 812
NOWELL,
  DEMPSY, 891(2)

DEMPSY M., 892
FRANCES A., 892
IDA M., 892
JAMES A., 892
JAMES H.,
  891(2), 892
JOAB, 891
JOHN HENRY, 891

JOHN T., 892
MARY M., 892
NANNIE E., 892
SAMUEL A., 892
SAMUEL J., 891
NUNNELLY,
  ANNIE BALDWIN,

888

-O-

OAKS,
  ELIZABETH, 873
OATES,
  ROWENA, 913
O'CONNER,
  E. G., 824
  JAMES, 812, 829
O'CONNOR,
  ANNIE (JAMES),
    892
  GRATTAN E., 892
  JAMES, 830, 892
  KATHLEEN, 892
OLDHAM,
  MOSES, 804, 818
OLIVE,
  HOWELL, 895
  MARTHA J., 895
OLIVER,
  ALFRED, 830
O'NEAL,
  C. H., 877
  EMILY E., 895
  LABAN, 895
  MARGARET ANN

  JOHNSON,MRS.,
    877
  MARY
    (McLEMORE)JONES,

  879
PATRICK, 879
OTEY,
  BISHOP, 835
OVERTON,
  JOHN, 823
  SAMUEL B., 823
OZIER,
  GREEN G., 892
  MAUD L., 893
  ROY L., 893
  SAMUEL M., 892
  TERRY SAMUEL,

893
  WILLIAM, 892

-P-

PACE, -
  HENNING, 799
  HENRY, 819
PALMER,
  WIDOW, 900
PARDUE,
  ISAAC H., 893
  J. J., 893
  LAURA, 893
  ROSA L., 893
  SARAH (DAVIS),
    893
PARKER,
  A. H., 916
  DAVID H., DR.,
    893
  HENRY S., 893
  J. M., 883
  JENNIE, 883
  SARAH E., 894
  SUSAN F., 894
  SUSAN F.
    (PINKSTON), 893
  WM. L., 818
PARKHAM,
  W. H., 806
PARKS,
  JNO. M., 814
PARTON,
  W. K., 817
PATTERSON,
  ALLEN L., 852
  DRUCILLA, 852
  FRANCES, 852
PATTON,
  ALEXANDER, 810

  JAMES, 810
PATTON & TAYLOR,

  810
PAXTON,
  J.W., 816
PEARCEY,
  WM., 817
PEARCY,
  EVERETT, 825(2)
PEARSON,
  ELIZA
    (WILLIAMS), 894
  ETHEL M., 843
  J. D., 843(2)
  JAMES C., 894
  JOHN L., 894
  JOHN S., 894,
    895
  JONATHAN D.,
    HON., 894
  MARY E., 894

NANNIE E., 843,
  894
NEEDHAM B., 894
SEBAN W., 894
SIDNEY A., 843
WALTER L., 894
WILLIAM, 894(2)
WILLIAM M., 894
PEMBERTON,
  —, 896
PENDER,
  LEWIS, DR., 834
PENDLER,
  MATILDA COOR,
    MRS., 835
PENN,
  H. L., 843
  W. C., 826
PERKINS,
  G. G., 823
  G. S., 806
  JACOB, 834
  MARY
    DeLESSELEINE,
    913
  NEWTON C.,
    CAPT., 823
  SOPHIA, MRS.,
    834
PERRY, 810
  ----, 914
PERSON, 810
  —, 864
  B. R., 806
  B.R., 812
PERSON &
  CHRISTIAN, 810
PETTUS,
  HENRY L., REV.,
    831
PHILLIPS,
  ----, 827
  ALICE G., 895
  JAMES A., 895
  JAMES L., 895
  JOSEPH, 800, 807
  LIZZIE, 895
  LOU M., 895
  MARY E., 895
  MINERVA J., 895
  RADA, 895
  SARAH M., 895
  SWAINE H., 895
  THOMAS L., 895
  THOMAS P., 895
PIERCE,
  FRANKLIN, 892
PIERCY,
  CADER, 891
  HARRIET, 891(2)
PIKE,
  ALBERT, 816
PIRTLE,
  MALINDA, 865
PITTS,

-Z-